# Developing Teacher
# Expertise

**Also available from Bloomsbury**

*Assessment: A Practical Guide for Primary Teachers,* by Lyn Overall and
   Margaret Sangster
*Early Numeracy: Mathematical activities for 3 to 5-year-olds,* by Margaret
   Sangster and Rona Catterall
*Effective Teaching and Learning in Practice,* Don Skinner
*Philosophy of Education: An Introduction,* edited by Richard Bailey
*Primary Curriculum – Teaching the Core Subjects,* edited by Rosemary Boys
   and Elaine Spink
*Primary Curriculum – Teaching the Foundation Subjects,* edited by Rosemary
   Boys and Elaine Spink
*Primary Teacher's Handbook,* by Lyn Overall and Margaret Sangster
*Readings for Reflective Teaching,* edited by Andrew Pollard
*Reflective Teaching: Evidence-informed Professional Practice,* Andrew Pollard
*Secondary Teacher's Handbook,* by Lyn Overall and Margaret Sangster
*The Primary Teacher's Handbook (2nd edition),* Lyn Overall and Margaret
   Sangster

# Developing Teacher Expertise

## Exploring Key Issues in Primary Practice

Edited by
Margaret Sangster

B L O O M S B U R Y
LONDON • NEW DELHI • NEW YORK • SYDNEY

**Bloomsbury Academic**
An imprint of Bloomsbury Publishing Plc

50 Bedford Square
London
WC1B 3DP
UK

175 Fifth Avenue
New York
NY 10010
USA

www.bloomsbury.com

First published 2013

**British Library Cataloguing-in-Publication Data**
A catalogue record for this book is available from the British Library.

ISBN: HB:    978-1-4411-4096-8
       PB:    978-1-4411-7911-1

**Library of Congress Cataloging-in-Publication Data**
A catalog record for this book is available from the Library of Congress

Typeset by Fakenham Prepress Solutions, Fakenham, Norfolk NR21 8NN
Printed and bound in India

# Contents

List of contributors                                              ix
Preface                                                           xv
Introduction                                                      xvi

### Part I The Learning Environment

**1** **Do schools work – a challenge to the institutionalization
of learning?**
*Rebecca Austin*                                                   3

**2** **When does inclusion become exclusion for the rest of the
class?**
*Maggie Evans*                                                     7

**3** **Does differentiation make it easier for children to learn?**
*Jill Matthews*                                                   11

**4** **Why aim to create independent learners?**
*Margaret Sangster*                                               15

**5** **Why and how can we engage children with their learning?**
*Claire Hewlett*                                                  19

**6** **Can we use the built environment to support children's
learning?**
*Jonathan Barnes*                                                 23

**7** **What do we understand from using images in the classroom?**
*Peter Dorman*                                                          **27**

**8** **Do displays contribute to children's learning?**
*Bridie Price*                                                          **30**

**9** **Do interactive whiteboards support or reduce creativity in the classroom?**
*Karl Bentley*                                                          **34**

**10** **Is learning outside the classroom worth it?**
*Michael Green*                                                         **37**

**11** **What is the value of encouraging talk in your classroom?**
*Jill Matthews*                                                         **42**

**12** **Does rewarding children lead to independent learners?**
*Margaret Sangster*                                                     **47**

**Part II The Curriculum**

**13** **Should we be teaching a second language to children under seven?**
*Vikki Schulze and Anthony Clarke*                                      **53**

**14** **Is drama a luxury in the primary classroom?**
*Tracy Parvin*                                                          **57**

**15** **Is there a place for picture fiction with children over seven?**
*Susan Barrett*                                                         **61**

**16** Does correct spelling really matter?
*Caroline Tancock*                                             65

**17** Is it possible to make mathematics real and meaningful
in the classroom?
*Jon Wild*                                                     69

**18** How can questioning create thoughtful reflection
and learning in mathematics?
*Paula Stone*                                                  73

**19** Is physical education more than just being
physically active?
*Kristy Howells*                                               78

**20** Should ICT be taught as a subject, used as a learning
tool or is there a need for both?
*Nyree Scott*                                                  83

**21** Should children be learning to make art or learning
through art?
*Peter Gregory*                                                87

Part III  The Wider World

**22** Why do children and teachers need to develop a
multicultural and global perspective?
*Tony Mahon*                                                   93

**23** What makes stereotypes pernicious?
*Stephen Scoffham*                                             97

**24** Should we teach children about current affairs?
Stephen Scoffham
**100**

**25** Maps are increasingly being used by children but do these maps tell the truth?
Terry Whyte
**103**

### Part IV Teachers' Professional Status

**26** What are some philosophical, sociological and psychological perspectives on education?
Rosemary Walters
**109**

**27** What is meant by professional identity?
Vanessa Young
**113**

**28** What does professionalism mean for a teacher?
Peter Dorman
**117**

**29** Why should teachers be researchers?
Viv Wilson
**121**

**30** How do we improve our own practice?
Viv Wilson
**125**

**31** How can mentors and mentees make the most of the mentoring process?
Donna Birrell
**128**

Endnote
**132**
Index
**133**

# List of contributors

**Rebecca Austin** worked in primary schools in Kent, UK, before becoming Senior Lecturer in Primary English at Canterbury Christ Church University, UK, promoting children's literature as central to children's development as readers, writers and talkers. Her research interests include learning outside the classroom and the use of popular culture in schools. She is currently studying and researching the role of the media in adolescents' identity formation.

**Jonathan Barnes** has 30 years' classroom experience and a love of the arts, which power his commitment to cross-curricular approaches. As a headteacher, he devised a curriculum based on the school locality. He is a Senior Lecturer at Canterbury Christ Church University, UK, and researches links between cross-curricular/creative approaches and well-being. He is the author of *Cross-Curricular Learning 3–14* (2011) and now teaches about exploring the environment as well as music in education.

**Susan Barrett** is Senior Lecturer at Canterbury Christ Church University, UK, and lectures in primary English and professional studies as well as link tutoring students in school. She has worked in a secondary and a number of primary schools before taking up a post in higher education. Her particular interests are in the teaching of poetry in schools, children's literature and how we develop as writers.

**Karl Bentley** is an Associate Lecturer at Canterbury Christ Church University, UK, and lectures in ICT, science, maths and professional studies as well as link tutoring students in school. He was a school-based ICT advanced skills teacher before entering higher education. His main interests are the development of the Primary Curriculum and the use of interactive technologies to deliver university course content.

**Donna Birrell** is Senior Lecturer at Canterbury Christ Church University, UK, and currently lectures in professional studies and primary music. She also has a particular interest in mentoring students and maintaining effective

X List of contributors
X  List of contributors

partnerships with schools. Since entering higher education she has always prioritized this aspect of her work and is interested in how both mentors and students can gain the most from the process.

**Anthony Clarke** is Senior Lecturer at Canterbury Christ Church University, UK, where he lectures in professional studies and primary languages and manages several exchange programmes with universities across Europe. He has been both a deputy headteacher and a headteacher in primary schools in Kent, UK, and has a particular interest in international education systems and developing students' language and cultural awareness. He works closely with local schools as a link tutor and provides support for the development of primary languages.

**Peter Dorman** has had a long and varied career in primary education, working in schools and for local education authorities, and is currently Principal Lecturer at Canterbury Christ Church University, UK. He teaches ICT and professional studies but is also involved in the cross-curricular module. His interests include the effective use of ICT with pupils with additional educational needs, learning in global contexts and the professional development of newly qualified teachers.

**Maggie Evans** has worked in a variety of settings, including preschool, infant, primary, further and higher education and did a stint in prison education. She has taught teacher education modules on diversity and participation and professional studies at Canterbury Christ Church University, UK. Currently, she is Deputy Headteacher of an inclusive primary school and nursery with responsibility for special educational needs.

**Peter Gregory** is Senior Lecturer at Canterbury Christ Church University, UK, and previously taught across all phases and sectors of education in London and the southeast. He originally trained in ceramics before teaching in a number of schools and other settings. He held several school leadership and local authority advisory roles before teaching on a range of ITE programmes in London and Kent. He is an enthusiastic member of the National Society of Education in Art and Design (NSEAD) and the International Society for Education through Art (InSEA).

**Michael Green** is the Programme Director for the BA in Primary Education at Canterbury Christ Church University, UK, but also leads the undergraduate work on learning outside the classroom. His interests include children's use of technology and the opportunities and barriers for children to learn outside the classroom. Prior to joining initial teacher education he was an assistant headteacher in a large primary school in Medway.

**Claire Hewlett** comes from a background of teaching in primary schools. As Senior Lecturer at Canterbury Christ Church University, UK, she now lectures in primary art, science, cross-curricular approaches and professional studies. She is particularly interested in how art can be used to support learning across all areas of the curriculum, particularly how art can be used as a vehicle for children to express their wider learning and understanding. She believes in taking an active learning approach to teaching.

**Kristy Howells** is Senior Lecturer at Canterbury Christ Church University, UK, where she lectures in primary physical education and professional studies as well as link tutoring students in school nationally and internationally. She currently leads on a part-time primary education programme specializing in the seven to eleven age range and lectures on the physical education and sports sciences degree course. Her particular area of research expertise is physical activity.

**Tony Mahon** is Senior Lecturer at Canterbury Christ Church University, UK, where he lectures in primary English, English as an Additional Language (EAL) and professional studies and also has responsibility for organizing international placements for student teachers. He has worked as a teacher and teacher educator in England, Egypt, Saudi Arabia, Philippines, Japan and Hong Kong and is currently a consultant for World Bank Projects in Palestine. His academic interests include the pedagogy of English as an additional language and multicultural and development education.

**Jill Matthews** is Senior Lecturer at Canterbury Christ Church University, UK, and has a leading management role on the undergraduate primary education programme. She has both secondary and primary teaching experience and, within the primary sector she has held subject responsibility posts for science, mathematics, literacy and primary languages. Her research interests include the role language plays in developing children's mathematical understanding and creating inclusive learning environments.

**Tracy Parvin** is Senior Lecturer at Canterbury Christ Church University, UK, and lectures in primary English and professional studies. She also link tutors students on their school practices. Having gained experience of working throughout the 5–11 age range, she has a particular interest in the development of reading. More recently, she is engaged in activities which explore how teachers might tap into children's natural enthusiasm for storytelling.

**Bridie Price** is a Senior Lecturer at Canterbury Christ Church University, UK, and lecturers in primary mathematics, art and professional studies. She also runs support workshops for students prior to entering their school practice. She has taught in primary schools in London and Kent over a period of more than 20 years. Her current research interests include the use of display in the learning environment and developing mathematical understanding through the use of story.

**Margaret Sangster** was a Principal Lecturer at Canterbury Christ Church University, UK, where she lectured in primary mathematics and professional studies as well as link tutoring students in school. She has worked in a number of primary and middle schools before entering higher education where she has held several management posts. Her particular interests are students' mathematical subject knowledge, teachers' classroom practice, independent learners and children's ability to develop investigative skills.

**Vikki Schulze** is Senior Lecturer at Canterbury Christ Church University, UK, where she lectures in primary languages and professional studies. She also link tutors students in schools in the UK and in Germany. As an active member of the primary language team, she is involved in an extensive exchange scheme of teacher trainees across several European countries. She has taught across the 5–11 age range in a number of primary schools before entering higher education. Her particular interests are pupil motivation and integrating languages into the wider curriculum.

**Stephen Scoffham** has a reputation as an advisor/consultant for school atlases as well as for his work on primary school geography. His interests include creativity, sustainability, environmental education and global perspectives. He is Principal Lecturer at Canterbury Christ Church University, UK, and teaches on geography and global modules. With Jonathan Barnes, he has been a leading light in the work on neurology and education. Stephen is currently the Geographical Association's Publications' Officer and a trustee of a local development education centre (WEDG).

**Nyree Scott** is Senior Lecturer at Canterbury Christ Church University, UK, and lecturers in primary ICT, mathematics and professional studies as well as link tutoring students in school. She is involved in running a part-time flexible learning route, which involves considerable use of modern technology. She worked in a small primary school with a mixed class before entering higher education. Her particular interests are looking at how ICT can be embedded across the curriculum and how it can be tracked and assessed.

**Paula Stone** is Senior Lecturer at Canterbury Christ Church University, UK, where she teaches primary mathematics education at both undergraduate and postgraduate level, with particular responsibility for the mathematics research module. She is an associate of the NCETM and contributes regularly to publications including writing for *Primary Magazine*. Paula also works part-time on a consultancy basis supporting mathematics leadership in schools in Kent, UK.

**Caroline Tancock** is a Senior Lecturer and member of the BA (Hons) in Primary Education management team at Canterbury Christ Church University, UK. She teaches many modules on the undergraduate programme, including English and professional studies, and the full-time PGCE English course. Her current research interests include cultural influences on reading experiences and attitudes.

**Karen Vincent** worked as a teacher for 18 years before taking up a post in the Primary Education department at Canterbury Christ Church University, UK, where she is Senior Lecturer. She teaches both undergraduates and postgraduates, specializing in early years education. She also teaches professional studies and link tutors students on their school placements. Her research interests include young children's perceptions of learning and the transition between Year R and Year 1 (4–6-year-olds).

**Rosemary Walters** has a background in teaching religious education and history and has been a local authority religious education support teacher and a cathedral schools officer before working with primary ITE students focusing on these two subject areas. She is now Senior Lecturer at Canterbury Christ

Church University, UK, and has a special interest in the role of spiritual development and the concept of transformative education.

**Terry Whyte** is Senior Lecturer at Canterbury Christ Church University, UK, where he lectures in primary geography, global studies and professional studies as well as link tutoring students in school. He chairs one of the regional partnership groups that meet to discuss students' school experiences. He has worked in a number of primary schools before entering higher education. His interests are students' understanding and awareness of their environment and the world around them and developing children's geographical skills.

**Jon Wild** is Senior Lecturer at Canterbury Christ Church University, UK, where he lectures in primary mathematics and ICT as well as supporting students in school as a link tutor. He has spent 19 years working in primary schools, culminating in the post of headteacher, before entering higher education. Part of his role at Canterbury Christ Church University is to raise the profile of men joining primary education programmes. His particular research interest is how to use ICT to develop and extend children's mathematical understanding.

**Viv Wilson** is a Principal Lecturer at Canterbury Christ Church University, UK, where she lectures in research methods and professional studies. She has worked in primary and secondary schools before entering higher education as a lecturer in educational drama. She has considerable experience of working in international teacher training settings. Her current interests include mentoring, students' professional learning in schools and supporting teachers as school-based researchers.

**Vanessa Young** is a Senior Lecturer at Canterbury Christ Church University, UK, where she lectures in primary music and professional studies and has held the role of Director on a highly regarded 7–14 teacher training programme. She has a particular interest in the curriculum and the aims of education. She has worked in a number of primary schools and also has extensive experience in staff development. Her writing and research focus on aspects of teacher development.

# Preface

What are the issues that education raises for you? Beyond the technical skills and knowledge aspects of education, teachers and student teachers face questions that challenge their beliefs and approaches to their teaching and learning. This book contains a series of short chapters that ask why you do what you do. The authors ask you, the reader, to reflect on your own practice and challenge your beliefs about how and what you teach.

The contributors, all tutors in the primary department at Canterbury Christ Church University, UK, are deeply engaged in primary education and not only enjoy discussions with students and teachers but also actively pursue research and writing about primary education. When I suggested that we write a collection worthy of discussion, I immediately received a flood of topics that they wished to write about and raise as issues with their students and the teachers they work with. They strongly believe that teachers should be reflective and reflexive professionals and that children will benefit from teachers who continue to develop their practice throughout their career. To enable this to happen it is important to be aware of the view of others and to ask oneself challenging questions about one's own practice.

The contributors agreed that short, but focused articles would be ideal as pre-reading as well as follow-up reading to seminars, tutorials or discussions. Often, as tutors, mentors and teachers, we cast around for suitable short articles to initiate thinking about topics covered in sessions or issues that arise in the classroom. This book seeks to provide stimulating starting points for reflection and further research.

Some of the really interesting discussions are only hinted at. The articles are designed to provide challenge to your thinking. They inform but also raise questions, the intention being to promote debate. Many of these are the questions that are raised in education today, have been raised in the past and will be continue to be raised in the future, so they really can be described as contemporary. Informed discussion is a powerful way to encourage people to become reflective practitioners and the papers, it is to be hoped, will prompt debate as well as lead you into further enquiry.

# Introduction

Teachers and students bring many talents to their role in the classroom and will have expertise in several aspects of their teaching. Good teachers can be remarkably different in their style of teaching and the talents and knowledge they bring to the classroom so it is difficult to conceive of the definitive 'expert teacher'. The best we can do is to develop our understanding of our professional role and aim to be effective as possible in getting children to learn.

Alexander in his report on primary school education *Children, their World, their Education* (2010, pp. 408–19) discusses the evolution of beliefs about expertise in the classroom. The variation in expectations in recent years is considerable but there appears to be consensus on the competences required to teach and that good subject knowledge is required. These competences are possibly best captured by the standards required for qualified teacher status (TDA, 2007) in which 33 competences must be achieved before you may teach in an English state-run school.

These standards set a baseline but do they capture the qualities for the effective teacher? In Alexander's team's research, they identified the belief that good teachers work within a complex matrix of head, heart, child and subject knowledge. Evans (2011) also describes a gulf between the 'demanded' professionalism shaped by the required competencies and the 'enacted' profes-sionalism required by practising teachers. She believes that true professionals create their own teacher identity within and despite the confines of policy and context and good teachers have 'emotional ownership' of their role. This view of emotional and intellectual ownership is shared by Malm (2009) who suggests we need to pay more attention to the personal aspects of teacher development, recognizing its contribution to professional development.

In the belief that development of and beyond the competences is best met through reading and discourse, the short chapters in this book aim to challenge your thinking on your classroom practice as well as offering potential for further study through the references to theory and research. Not all the issues raised in this book have resolution; they remain your decision; but after reflection we hope that you will make an informed decision grounded in your educational beliefs. Knowing you have explored the issues, it will allow you to be more confidence in your decisions as a professional practitioner.

Each contributor has chosen to write about an issue that for them raises questions. It is to be hoped, they will raise questions for you too about your own practice. Whether the chapters prompt you to read further or discuss the issues with colleagues, you will know a little bit more about education and possibly about your stance on educational issues.

The book is divided into four parts; the learning environment, the curriculum, the wider world and teachers' professional status. However, it would have been possible to place some chapters in several of the parts. For example, when asking whether maps tell the truth, which has been placed in the wider world section, it could just as easily have been placed in the curriculum section or the learning environment section. Therefore, we hope you will not be restricted by the headings or even the questions set by the titles. We would wish your debates to be wide ranging and embedded in your own experience as much as the words of others.

# The learning environment

Part I, The learning environment, opens with a big question; Rebecca Austin asks, 'Do schools work?' Possibly, we are used to being part of the system, we have grown up with the ways in which schools operate and are happy to perpetuate a system that worked for us. But society and the world is a rapidly changing environment. We only have to look back in time to see how different people's lives are today from 10 years ago. So it is a valid question to ask whether we are providing the right educational experience for our young children who will be emerging into a very different adult world from the one we currently experience. Education operates in a framework of legislation and government priorities but that should not prevent teachers from reflecting on their own actions. For example, the government promotes inclusion and it is undoubtedly a worthy educational aim but Maggie Evans asks the practical questions which are resultant for the class teacher. Individual teachers' actions are to a great extent driven by their beliefs. What is your pedagogic approach to these issues?

Having set the scene for how the whole school functions, the chapters that follow, examine and question different aspects of teacher practice in the classroom. Not all education systems in the world choose to differentiate their teaching. There are many models being used in practice, whole-class teaching, personalized learning, individual learning from structured programmes, setting, streaming and group work to name a few. Differentiation is currently a dominant practice in English primary schools. Jill Matthews asks us to think more deeply about this practice.

Margaret Sangster tackles a topic that has been asked for many years and one still has to question, in the current English education climate, whether we are any nearer succeeding in creating independent citizens capable of managing and initiating their own learning? She particularly asks whether the actions in our own classrooms truly promote independence or dependency on the teacher. This theme is nicely developed in Claire Hewlett's contribution on active learning in which she promotes the need for children to engage practically in their learning. Will this approach improve children's ability to learn? Complementing Claire's paper is Jonathan Barnes practical suggestions for ways of promoting active learning with children. He offers tried and tested approaches to providing a creative curriculum based on his extensive work with trainee teachers, teachers and children.

After this trio of articles comes an intriguing and original paper by Peter Dorman about the use of images in the classroom. This is particularly relevant today as the internet offers a window on the wider world and creates an immediate link to current affairs and other lives. This aspect of global images could be nicely linked to the papers by Tony Mahon and Stephen Scoffham in the wider world section where they discuss multiculturalism, globalization, stereotypes and current affairs. This is a good example of how education has changed significantly in recent years and Peter is quite right to ask us what effect this change has on our practice as primary teachers. Also linked to this paper is Bridie Price's discussion on classroom and school display. There are primary schools in other countries that have no displays on their classroom walls and see no educational value in displaying children's work or instructional material. Looking round the world, there are few classrooms as well adorned as those in England. Why do we as teachers do this? It takes time and care. What purpose does it serve? A third paper in this group is Karl Bentley's discussion on the use of interactive whiteboards. Are we really using all they offer? Karl suggests possibly not and is particularly keen to ask about how teachers use them as a resource and a tool for learning.

In recent years there has been recognition of the contribution learning outside the classroom can make to children's learning. Whereas the internet can bring the outside in to the classroom, Michael Green questions the value of taking children out. There are valid educational reasons for offering children experiential learning and taking them into different working environments but do we make the most of these educational visits and what do the children learn from them? They are time consuming so can their place in the curriculum be justified?

The last two chapters in this part are about pedagogic choices; exploring the role of children's talk and a challenge to the practice of rewarding children. How much talking is acceptable and what is its purpose? These are questions teachers frequently ask of their own practice and Jill Matthews gives the reader an opportunity to reflect on this in the context of the views of others. Rewarding children is a common practice in English primary schools but have we considered the short- and long-term consequences of having a strong reward system established in the classroom? Finally in this part, Margaret Sangster asks if such reward systems lead to self-motivation and independent learning or continue a culture of dependency and how much reward is behaviour management and how much the promotion of good work?

# The curriculum

Part II examines aspects of the curriculum. The potential for writing about curriculum issues is vast, with each subject having unique challenges. This part holds only a sample of these issues but hopefully, the way in which the issues are considered and discussed can be transferred to other aspects or other subjects. In this way, they address the specific but offer a prompt to examine other curriculum approaches. Again, this part opens with a challenge to national policy with a very thought-provoking paper by Anthony Clarke and Vikki Schultz. They ask why we, in England, are not teaching younger children a second language. They present a strong case for starting second language teaching with five-year-olds. As tutors who have experienced primary education in several European countries and who realize that most Europeans are bilingual, they raise a good question. We are well aware that most children have poor second-language abilities in England and they put a strong case for introducing second-language teaching at a much earlier age. What do you think?

This opener is followed by three chapters on aspects of teaching English. The first is a consideration of the value of drama by Tracy Parvin. As there is a current government enthusiasm for the basics in primary education, any but the core subjects is under threat of marginalization. Drama is an aspect of the core subject of English so Tracy asks us if its continued presence can be justified. This is followed by a passionate plea for picture fiction in Key Stage 2 (7–11-year-olds). While this discussion is about Key Stage 2, the justification presented by Susan Barrett could be equally applied to Key Stage 1 (5–7 years). Even as an adult, an illustration adds so much complementary information to the text. I recently heard someone describing how he learned to read through his enthusiasm for the Rupert Bear comic strip. How the pictures took him into the speech and finally into the prose beneath, each telling the story in a different but similar way. How dull life would be without illustrations but also how important a part do they play in reading? This chapter could easily be linked to Peter Dorman's and Bridie Price's contributions on image and display in Part 1. A final challenge is offered by Caroline Tancock who asks if correct spelling really matters. She explores how children learn spelling and asks us to reflect on how closely this matches are own teaching approaches.

Moving from one core subject to another, mathematics, there are two chapters written by Jon Wild and Paula Stone. Jon asks whether it is possible to make maths real and meaningful in the classroom. Many children find maths difficult. This is possibly because it becomes symbolic and abstract fairly quickly. Jon would argue that creating contexts that have meaning for the children will help them understand the maths. Others would argue there is evidence that contexts confuse children and that they bring commonsense solutions to maths problems and as a consequence failure. Is maths another language in a world with its own rules? The answer to that is probably yes; in this case, how should we teach it? Do you agree with Jon's argument? Paula raises very interesting points about ways to use questions in mathematics so that children are engaged in mathematical thinking. This is a powerful paper for mathematics teaching but also for teaching any subject. It is an excellent example of how thinking about the way we teach in one subject can be transferred to other subjects. She really challenges our teaching style in relation to challenging children's thinking.

A rising profile in primary school is that of educating children to be healthy. Kristy Howells opens the discussion on the role physical education lessons play in this debate. This is an area that looks as if it will increase in importance as we pay more attention to the 'whole child', an approach instigated by 'Every Child Matters' and furthered through the 'Children's Plan' in England.

Nyree Scott's chapter on ICT could have been placed alongside Karl Bentley's on interactive whiteboards, so you may choose to read them together. Nyree's question is about the role of ICT in the primary classroom. It is a National Curriculum subject therefore should it be a subject in its own right? Is this the way it is taught in schools? Others would see it as a resource to be employed in the teaching of other subjects. What are we doing in the classroom? It is inevitable that the presence of ICT in the classroom will increase alongside the use of technology in society. In which case, how schools use ICT is an important question. Remembering that we are teaching the citizens of the future, how would you position yourself on the use of ICT in your classroom? A similar question is raised by Peter Gregory in a different context. He is asking whether children should be making art or appreciating it. Both papers are linked by questioning the children's level of practical engagement with the subject, as does Karl's earlier paper. Is this a question of position or balance?

# The wider world

This is a small but challenging part, containing four key discussions. It opens with Tony Mahon discussing the roles of multiculturalism and globalization in the Primary Curriculum in the context of increasing global awareness. For many schools, multiculturalism is a daily reality and there is some excellent practice that addresses the needs of children from many backgrounds. In other schools, it is a debate that has yet to occur as the school population is homogeneously white and of English ancestry. This is unlikely to continue in a country that considers itself multicultural. This is a topic that can be discussed far more easily in a theoretical context but needs to be considered far more practically. It is hard for teachers to put themselves in the shoes of others and reflect on the implications of their actions on children from other cultural backgrounds, but it must be done. Is this chapter a starting point for reflection and action? The theme of global awareness is carried through into the next contribution, from Stephen Scoffham.

Stephen Scoffham is greatly concerned with how primary schools address global issues and his two chapters are derived from his work in this area. He asks two challenging questions; what makes stereotypes pernicious and should we teach children about current affairs? When you look at geography textbooks from the past, we see countries represented in ways that are quite alarming to us today. A native African standing with a spear outside a mud hut is not the way Africans live and dress today and yet these images persist in school. No doubt there is an intention to capture difference and tradition but this could be considered a negative stereotype. The cultures of the world are converging and differences are subtle. What should we be teaching primary children? In his chapter on images, Peter Dorman offers further thoughts on stereotyping and these two chapters could be read together. Stephen's other concern is for the depressing nature of the media. While it is good to bring the outside in, is it too devastating for young children? Much of the media are about sensationalism, war and natural disaster. Should we be coping with these issues and, if yes, how?

Terry Whyte has contributed the final chapter in this part. Again, the sense of change in primary school teaching is present as he discusses the increased use of maps in the classroom and to what extent they give us an interpreted view of the world. As children were we aware that Britain featured near the centre of most world maps and are you old enough to remember the bright pink colouring of empire? How much did those map projections enhance the importance of colonial domination? There is plenty of food for thought here.

# Teachers' professional status

This part could have been placed first but it possibly has more value at the end, particularly if you have had the opportunity to reflect on some of the previous chapters. We hope you will have concluded that there are many things to argue about in primary education and that the teacher or student in the classroom has a powerful say in how children are taught, even within the parameters of legislation and policy. Your beliefs about education will permeate everything you do in the classroom, consciously or subconsciously. This part considers what it is to be a professional teacher in a series of closely complementary chapters.

The discussion begins with Rosemary Walters taking the traditional subjects of philosophy, sociology and psychology to challenge our thinking about the purpose of education. This is followed by Vanessa Young's chapter on professional identity. Many people consider themselves to be professional or to have a job that is a profession. Each has a body of knowledge or expertise that makes them in demand and often respected by others. It is important to examine what exactly a professional identity is in relation to teaching, which Vanessa does. Peter Dorman takes this a step further in considering what implications this has for individuals in the teaching profession.

Throughout the book each chapter has explored topics that require decision making either on an ideological or a practical level. These decisions are driven by policy and beliefs – your beliefs. No doubt these beliefs will alter as you progress through your career. It is vital that you do evolve and develop your practice. The world around you is not standing still and a good teacher will be aware and adapt to change. Viv Wilson questions whether a good way for this to happen is through researching your own practice and follows this with a broader approach to improving your own practice.

The final chapter deserves its place as the last word. The book has been a consideration of aspects of practice that offer an opportunity to consider your own professional beliefs and decision making. Donna Birrell asks you to consider your role as a learner or mentee and your role as a teacher of children and students or mentor. This is a good place to finish the book but also to hope that for you, it is an opportunity to further your professional development and to hone your expertise as a teacher.

# References

Alexander, R. (ed.) (2010) *Children, their World, their Education*, Abingdon: Routledge

Department for Education (DfE) (2003) *Every Child Matters* – a green paper presented to Parliament, September 2003, London: HMSO

Department for Education (DfE) (2007) *The Children's Plan: building brighter futures* London: DfE

Evans, L. (2011) 'The "shape" of teacher professionalism in England: professional standards, performance management, professional development and the changes proposed in the 2010 White Paper', *British Educational Research Journal*, 37:5, 851–70)

Malm, B. (2009) 'Towards a new professionalism: enhancing personal and professional development in teacher education', *Journal of Education for Teaching*, 35:1, 77–91

Teacher Development Agency (2007, revised 2008) *Qualifying to Teach*, London: TDA (a further revision will come into force in September 2012)

# Part I
## The Learning Environment

1 Do schools work – a challenge to the institutionalization of learning? 3

2 When does inclusion become exclusion for the rest of the class? 7

3 Does differentiation make it easier for children to learn? 11

4 Why aim to create independent learners? 15

5 Why and how can we engage children with their learning? 19

6 Can we use the built environment to support children's learning? 23

7 What do we understand from using images in the classroom? 27

8 Do displays contribute to children's learning? 30

9 Do interactive whiteboards support or reduce creativity in the classroom? 34

10 Is learning outside the classroom worth it? 37

11 What is the value of encouraging talk in your classroom? 42

12 Does rewarding children lead to independent learners? 47

It is important that teachers set up a good learning environment for the children in their class. This will involve the physical setting, the social and the emotional setting as well as providing intellectual stimulus. Part I contains chapters that reflect on some of the ways in which the learning environment can be established and influenced by the teacher.

# Do schools work – a challenge to the institutionalization of learning?

Rebecca Austin

**1**

What are you really good at? Is there a sport at which you excel? A language you speak fluently? Are you really knowledgeable about a particular topic? Are you creative? Are you an independent thinker? Are you self-motivated?

*Did you learn any of this in school?*

I am willing to bet that if you are truly fluent in another language you have learned it most through regular use outside school lessons; if you are good at sport that this, too, has been achieved through extracurricular activities such as membership of a club or group. Your hobbies and interests outside school are probably what you have most enthusiasm and interest in learning more about and getting better at – even if interests are triggered by something at school, the pursuit of those interests probably happens outside school. And what of those 'life skills'? Can you pinpoint school as the driving force behind your capacity to be creative, independent, self-motivated?

*Then what did you learn in school?*

Ivan Illich, in 1971, suggested that: 'Pupils do most of their learning without, and often despite, their teachers' (p. 28). Your responses to these questions may well bear personal testament to this. Illich's book is called *Deschooling Society* and he is one of a number of scholars who believe that schools are not fit for purpose; that our current approach to schooling is stuck in its beginnings in Victorian society and that children are being failed (and therefore *labelled* as failures) by a system that paradoxically claims to be (and, indeed, should be) empowering (see Holt, 1964; Claxton, 2010; Robinson and Gerver, 2010; Kohn, 2011).

In 1916 John Dewey wrote *Democracy and Education*. In it, he described the need for societies to pass on the skills and knowledge that they accrue. Initially, in simple cultures, says Dewey, these skills and knowledge can be learned incidentally through interactions with others within the usual life of the society. You learn to hunt by going hunting with others; you learn to build by building with others; you learn to talk by talking with others. You also learn the value and worth of these activities and why you need to know how to participate in them. However, Dewey suggests that, as societies become more complex, a formal system of education is required to transmit the 'resources and achievements' (p. 5) that have been amassed over time. The problem, as Dewey saw it, is that transferring learning to a formal context such as a 'school' detaches it from the 'personal and vital' (p. 6) aspects of learning as a natural part of social life.

In addition, over time, schooled learning or 'being educated' becomes an end in itself (Article 28 of the United Nations Convention on Children's Rights (1989) states:

'All children have the right to a primary education, which should be free' and the outcomes of education – such as levels in national tests (SATs) and GCSE and degree certificates – become a means by which the success of schools, institutions and individuals can be measured and judged. High value is placed on these measures of educational achievement and testing thus becomes one of the most important political tools that governments can use to push forward educational agendas – because governments, too, are judged by the educational success of those they govern (Ball, 2008). Children are then inevitably positioned in a deficit model – any who do not achieve what they should by the age they should, as dictated by the institutionalization of learning, are not successes. For John Holt, however, schools fail pupils far beyond the failure to enable them to succeed in tests. Most children, he says:

> fail to develop more than a tiny part of the tremendous capacity for learning, understanding and creating with which they were born and of which they made full use during, the first two or three years of their lives. (1964, p. 1)

The politicization of education, including the emphasis on testing, has had a profound effect on what happens in classrooms. Activities undertaken in school are frequently remote from activities undertaken in the real world and the process of learning is made abstract and de-contextualized. Children are given worksheets on 'calculations with money' rather than being given money to spend; they play in sand and water trays as a substitute for a visit to the beach; they write because they are told to, not because they have something to say (Grave, 1994).

*How real is your classroom? What is possible?*

Popular culture, electronic communication forms, social networking, television and games consoles – those things that consume children's real lives are barely touched on at school – these are not seen to be the things that constitute learning in school (Lambirth, 2003) and they are certainly not on the testing agenda. But they are the fibre of children's existence in the world – haven't they the right to learn about, with and through them (Marsh and Millard, 2000)?

As well as what is taught, schools situate these learning experiences within a false reality, with concomitant rules and expectations, particularly related to how children should behave and act. All children need to adapt their behaviour to fit with the requirements of school and for some children this means learning a whole new set of rules or 'ways of being' (Meek, 1991). Children who challenge or question the rules are frequently seen as trouble-makers or a problem in school because they don't fit school's rigid structures and because schools don't meet their needs. Schools take the world and all its wonders and squeeze it into the constraints of a curriculum that dictates what children should learn, at what age they should learn it and how and where they should learn it (Robinson, 2011). No wonder, for some or perhaps many children, this does not lead them to inspired learning or docile participation.

Alfie Kohn writing about 'feel-bad' education wonders what historians will make of contemporary approaches to education:

> What were we thinking, they will ask, shaking their heads, when we begrudged children the right to spend their days in a place which provides deep satisfactions and occasional giggles? How did we allow this to happen? (2011, p. 151)

*What do you want for the children in your class? How will you, as a primary school teacher, make school work for the children you teach?*

# References and further reading

Ball, S. (2008) *The Education Debate*, Bristol: The Policy Press

Claxton, G. (2010) *What's the Point of School? Rediscovering the heart of education*, London: Oneworld Publications

Dewey, J. (1916/2004) *Democracy and Education*, New Delhi: Cosmo Publications

Grave, D. (1994) *A Fresh Look at Writing*, Portsmouth: Heinemann

Holt, J. (1964) *How Children Fail*, New York: Dell

Illich, I. (1971/2002) *Deschooling Society*, London: Marion Boyars Publishers LtdKohn, A. (2011) *Feel-Bad Education: contrarian essays on children and schooling*, London: Beacon Press

Lambirth, A. (2003) '"They get enough of that at home": understanding aversion to popular culture in schools', *Reading*, 37, 9–13Marsh, J. and Millard, E. (2000) *Literacy and Popular Culture: using children's culture in the classroom*, London: Paul ChapmanMeek, M. (1991) *On Being Literate*, London: Bodley Head

Robinson, K. (2011) *Changing Education Paradigms*, RSA Animate (video) available at: http://ahrengot.com/opinions/our-school-system-is-broken/ (accessed August 2011)

Robinson, K. and Gerver, R. (2010) *Creating Tomorrow's Schools Today. Education – our children – their future*, London: Continuum

# When does inclusion become exclusion for the rest of the class?

## 2

### Maggie Evans

In England, where children with additional needs are educated has always been a topic for debate. From Warnock (HMSO, 1978) onwards, government policy has been consistent in requiring all schools to be inclusive, while recognizing that there will be some children for whom specialist provision is more appropriate. The interpretation of this thinking has varied from place to place and the picture across the country is of a wide variety in the amount of specialist provision on offer and the amount of support offered to mainstream schools and individual teachers. Some special schools have closed, others have changed designation and private providers have, in some areas, started to offer alternative establishments. Between 1979 and 1991, the number of children in special schools fell by nearly 30 per cent. It can be difficult for teachers to see how the inclusion agenda works in his/her classroom, taking into account national directives, local authority initiatives, their own school ethos and parental wishes. Some parents of children with additional needs are desperate for specialist provision for their children, other parents are equally desperate to keep their children in mainstream education.

*What is your experience and view of education being wholly inclusive?*

The Audit Commission (2002) found that in England and Wales, the proportion of children with statements in mainstream showed huge variations: in England, 15 per cent of primary schools had 3 per cent or more of pupils with statements, in Wales the figure is 27 per cent. The same report noted that a pupil with a statement in Lambeth was more than six times as likely to be in a special school than a pupil in Newham (10 miles away). Classroom practice in these two boroughs of London might, therefore, look very different, one from the other. Conclusions reached from these data might, however, lead thinkers in different directions:

> Some highly inclusive schools have a lower level of statements than one would expect, because they are more experienced at meeting children's needs. (Audit Commission, 2002)

*How much specialist provision, via special schools, and outreach support, does your local authority offer? Is there a postcode lottery element to this, in relation to neighbouring authorities?*

School effectiveness has been seen as the key to achievement for all, in contrast to the view of individual needs being met via a personalized curriculum, which has long been the language of special schools although personalized learning is also expected now in mainstream education. Teachers in mainstream are currently required to deliver both, an all-embracing curriculum and individual education plans.

*Is this dual delivery a possibility? Consider how the two demands might be implemented in your classroom.*

Sometimes it is easy to state general intentions such as 'I run an inclusive classroom' but specific situations can raise decision dilemmas for the teacher. For example, consider the following two situations. *What would you do?*

Scenario 1: Your year group studies the Tudors and visits Hampton Court every year. The cost has remained fairly constant. This year, you need to pay for a coach that will accommodate your wheelchair-using pupil. The cost is increased by £85. What will you do?

1 Ask the school leaders to dip into the school budget?
2 Ask all parents to pay more? (Some will undoubtedly object.)
3 Ask the parents of the wheelchair user to drive her and meet you there?

Scenario 2: A pupil with ADHD has, of late, been very agitated, possibly due to changes in his medication regime. You and your teaching assistant have devised an effective strategy in which the pupil has regular 15-minute breaks to run around the playground, use the adventure playground and play ball, for five minutes each time. Your assistant headteacher complains that your progress grids show that your least able group is making little progress in maths and literacy. The intervention work you have devised for this group is delivered by your teaching assistant who is currently supervising the ADHD pupil.

*What would you do?*

One factor in the brave new world is the number of adults with whom teachers work in the twenty-first century. Children with a high level of needs may be subject to inputs and evaluations from a range of professionals, including speech and language therapists, mental health workers, physiotherapists and others, all of whom have advice to offer, some of it conflicting. The role of the teacher is to sift this advice and to incorporate into everyday classroom life what is practicable.

Many programmes require the extra support offered by a support assistant, whose qualifications and experience are not regulated. The National College for School Leadership notes that between 2000 and 2009, the number of teachers was increased by 37,000, and the number of learning support assistants was increased by 100,000. Managing the training of other adults in the school is the responsibility of the senior managers, but stating these needs, and managing the input of these people is the class teacher's role. Effective deployment of well-trained assistants can transform life for all in the classroom and time for planning for this, in consultation with the SENCO, should be allocated. Careful differentiation and the planning for activities suited to each group should prevent what Ainscow (2000) describes in his observations of classroom practice: 'The helpers constant presence means that they [the students] faced fewer challenges.'

*What are your experiences and observations of how teachers deploy learning support assistants? Have you seen excellent practice, effective practice or poor practice?*

The 'hidden helper' in each classroom, widely used by teachers, is the peer group. Children under the age of eight tend to see the teacher's influence as the most important; after this age, the peer group is probably rated as more significant as a source of advice and support. Many adults will recall their knowledge about sex and relationships starting in the primary school playground! 'Buddying' or 'peer mentoring', particularly advised for children with emotional and behavioural difficulties, uses this fact to good effect: the buddy models social skills, in class and in the playground and is the child's champion. This strategy has had some positive results, particularly in relation to young people involved in antisocial behaviour outside of school.

*Can you see how you might use this idea? Do you feel that it might infringe the rights of the 'buddy' in enjoying unfettered playtimes? How do you think it might feel to be given a buddy?*

Jacqueline Wilson's books are a good source of reading to enter the world of the outsider and/or the recipient of perceived patronage.

So, is it worth the effort? David Blunkett, a cabinet minister between 1997 and 2005, overcame the twin disadvantages of extreme poverty and a visual impairment to spend a lifetime in politics, at the most influential levels. He did this through education via the University of Sheffield, after his special school suggested that he might be suited to a career as a lathe operator. Inclusive practices might mean that we are able to nurture future leaders so we need to use our influence wisely.

# References and further reading

Ainscow, M. (2000) 'Poor tactics let down mums' army', *Times Education Supplement*, 31 March

Audit Commission (2002) *Forget-Me-Not* report at www.audit.commission.gov.uk/ localgov/national-studies/pages/forgetmenot2002_copy.aspx

Booth, T. and Ainscow, M. (2002) *Index for Inclusion*, Canterbury: Centre for Studies in Inclusive Education

—*Breaking Down the Barriers* available at: www.csie.org/uk/publications/breaking-barriers.shtml (accessed Oct 2011)

Ellis, S., Tod, J. and Graham-Matheson, L. (2008) *Special Needs and Inclusion: reflection and renewal*, Birmingham: NASUWT

UNESCO (1994) *The Salamanca Statement and Framework for Action on Special Needs Education* adopted by the world conference on special educational needs, access and quality at Salamanca, Spain, June 1994, Madrid: UNESCo and Ministry of Education and Science

Warnock, M. (1978) *Warnock Report: special educational needs*, London: HMSO

# Does differentiation make it easier for children to learn?

## 3

Jill Matthews

The first of four main purposes of the National Curriculum (DfEE, 1999) is to establish an entitlement. The National Curriculum:

> secures for all pupils, irrespective of social background, culture, race, gender, differences in ability and disabilities, an entitlement to a number of areas of learning and to develop knowledge, understanding, skills and attitudes necessary for their self-fulfilment and development as active and responsible citizens. (p. 12)

But how is this achieved in practice? The dilemma for the teacher is twofold:

- whether to provide learning opportunities matched to their perception of a child's potential next learning steps
- or whether to facilitate an inclusive learning experience shared by all.

The first model is based on the teacher's perception of a child's potential next learning steps based on their knowledge of the child's prior experiences, prior performance and assessed level of skill and understanding, In the second approach, outcomes are expected to vary according to the individual child.

*From your experience, what do you think the strengths and limitations of both approaches might be?*

Learning is a complex phenomenon dependent on the learner's motivation and understanding and degree of difficulty of the experience. The motivation and interest of the learner determines the amount of effort and concentration they are prepared to invest in achieving that goal.

Tod and Ellis (2006) discuss the importance for setting appropriate learning challenges to promote inclusion. However, they appear to adhere to the principles of linear progression; one concept must be mastered before the next is tackled and that learning is reliant on a structured syllabus such as the National Curriculum and the Primary Framework. This could be regarded as the 'banking approach' to education (Freire, 1996) in line with model one just examined. Lucas and Claxton (2010), by way of contrast, argue that intelligence is expandable and suggest that schools should promote opportunities for learners to develop positive learning dispositions so that they can become flexible, creative and critical thinkers. Their view implies that learning occurs as needed within particular contexts and circumstances. This might best be served by model two. As Illeris (2007) so aptly puts it: 'The acquisition of knowledge without understanding is becoming increasingly inadequate in relation to the reality in which we live' (p. 74).

Consider the following two scenarios. How do you think the learning opportunities provided may have affected the motivation and potential achievement of the children? Is there evidence of planned differentiation to accommodate individual learning needs? What previous teaching and assessments may have informed the lesson and the learning environments?

Scenario 1: Following a stimulating introduction to the traditional stories genre, using a picture book, pairs of Year 4 children discussed and composed orally their own story starters with a focus on creating an atmospheric scene. The children were then sent back to grouped tables and asked to write a first draft of their story start, remembering to use 'exciting' words to draw their readers into the story. They were reminded to use the correct punctuation (capital letters, full stops and exclamation marks) and some of the phrases associated with the genre (Long, long ago; Once upon a time; Once; There was once, etc.), The teacher worked with a group of six children supporting them to develop their ideas as they wrote. A group of 10 children worked with a TA on a cloze procedure retelling the same story. Some work was recorded in writing in every child's book,

Scenario 2: A class of Year 5 children were asked to identify several skulls of animals found in the UK. They watched a short video clip of lions with a kill and gazelle grazing in Kenya. Working in friendship groups, they discussed the functions of their own teeth while munching on raw carrots and compared the teeth of the predators and grazers. The children then identified some of the skulls as belonging to herbivores or carnivores, finally identifying the animals as sheep, deer, rabbit, dog and cat. One large skull caused a problem because the children felt it did not belong to either of these two groups. Researching on the internet and in books from the library, they decided it was an omnivore. The TA made observation notes about how certain children contributed to the group discussion. The teacher circulated working for short intervals with groups as needed. The children chose how to record their decisions collaboratively. Some made annotations to photocopied diagrams or observational drawings, some created a PowerPoint and recorded their decisions using ICT. Others wrote up their decisions and justification in their logbooks.

*Compare the two scenarios by discussing the potential for motivation, learning and contextual understanding.*

The skill of the teacher lies in judging the balance between the learner's interests and motivation and their ability to achieve the new knowledge or skills, As Illeris (2007) suggests, the new learning or skills required by the task must not be too small to prevent any significant learning from taking place or so big that the task seems to be unachievable. If you accept Vygotsky's proposal that the level of potential development depends on collaborative interaction with a significant other or others and is initiated by cognitive challenge (Kozulin et al., 2003), learning is a 'social' experience. This experience might be with peers or the teacher. Thus, Mercer's model of subsequent 'intermental' thinking (Mercer, 2000), where teacher and learner stay attuned to one another's changing developing thinking, seems to be the most important factor in developing understanding. If this is so, interaction at the appropriate level becomes a significant factor in the learning process. Effective learning experiences require a relevant interesting context with opportunities for the learners to engage actively and collaboratively using language accessible to all participants.

*Do you agree with Vygotsky and Mercer and does this attune with your experience of children's learning?*

In countries where there is a practice of high stakes testing, teaching can move away from a focus on the learning needs of individual children towards a *teaching to the test* culture. This can encourage schools to group or set children according to their perceived ability, measured by test performance. Test performance is highly dependent on memorization and syllabi. This may narrow the learning opportunities for individual children, both by the time needed to memorise and the adherence to the syllabus. Little attention may be paid to understanding; learning experiences may become closed and simplified to enable children to achieve within the perceived capability of their teaching group and spontaneous opportunities ruled out. However, it could be argued that a secure body of knowledge and skills are acquired by the majority. Could this approach be an underlying cause of disaffection and create a sense of alienation for some children?

*How does this approach to education relate to contexts for effective learning discussed earlier?*

As a counter-example to the test performance approach, Finland, in 1985, abolished ability groups and the education system was characterized by uniformity, free education, free school meals and provision for special educational needs based on the principles of inclusion, primary and secondary school were combined and teachers stayed with their class for the first five years of school. There were no final examinations at the end of compulsory basic education (seven to sixteen years), pupils then attended a vocational school or institute or an academic high school. Exams or formal assessments were introduced at this stage. PISA (2009), the tri-annual survey that compares the end of compulsory education of students' acquired knowledge and skills essential for full participation in society, has consistently found Finnish pupils to achieve highly in literacy, mathematics and science compared to other European countries.

There are arguments for differentiating work and teaching the whole class, for setting and not setting. Maybe there are other 'differentiation' factors that are very important in facilitating learning. The conversations the teacher has with individual children, the listening to individuals, the assessment of individuals, the building on individual's prior knowledge and the opportunity to engage in social learning all appear to play a part. Effective differentiation is more than providing different tasks. It takes account of the individual, includes them in the social and purposeful co-construction of shared understanding. It recognizes and embraces individual difference and diversity.

*The next question is whether external pressures are allowed to compromise that process. What do you think?*

# References and further reading

DfEE (1999) *The National Curriculum*, London: HMSO

Ericsson, K. A. (2006) 'The influence of experience and deliberate practice on the development of superior expert performance', in Ericsson, K. A., Charness, N., Feltovich, P. J. and Hoffman, R. R. (eds) (2006) *The Cambridge Handbook of Expertise and Expert Performance*, Cambridge: Cambridge University Press

Freire, P. (1996) *The Pedagogy of the Oppressed*, London: Penguin

Illeris, K. (2007) *How we Learn – learning and non-learning in school and beyond*, London: Routledge

Kozulin, A., Gindis, B., Ageyev, V. S. and Miller, S. M. (2003) *Vygotsky's Educational Theory in Cultural Context*, Cambridge: Cambridge University Press

Lucas, B. and Claxton, G. (2010) *New Kinds of Smart*, Maidenhead: McGraw-Hill

Mercer, N. (2000) *Words and Minds: how we use language to think together*, London: Routledge

PISA (2009) available at: http://www.oecd.org/document/61/0,3746,en_32252351_32235731_46567613_1_1_1_1,00.html (accessed 22 August 2011)

Tod, J. and Ellis, S. (2006) 'Inclusive education', in Arthur, J., Grainger, T. and Wray, D. (eds) *Learning to Teach in the Primary School*, Abingdon: Routledge

# Why aim to create independent learners?

## Margaret Sangster

**4**

Teaching is generally considered to be effective when pupils spend considerable time on task, are intellectually challenged, receive a well-planned and structured curriculum where the work is well matched to individual ability and well monitored. This emerged in a comparative study of the findings of Oracle (1980), Bennett et al. (1984), Mortimer et al. (1988) and Alexander (1991) by Stevenson and Palmer in 1994. These targets will undoubtedly be met by the well-organized, dedicated teacher. It would suggest 'independent learning' is a goal that is supported by these factors but lies beyond them. It is a way of working that we hope children will carry forward into their lives. Most teachers would agree that education is more than getting children to store up a body of knowledge and skills. It is a complex business about helping children to become a successful part of society and culture.

*Do you think effective teaching encompasses independence as a goal or can it be effective without independence?*

'Just tell me what to do' is the plaintive cry of someone who has failed to understand the purpose of the task, lacks knowledge of how to engage and does not know how to seek ways forward. There is little ownership but there is recognition that the task needs to be completed. This, I would suggest, is the opposite of independent learning and promotes a culture of dependency.

To be independent requires confidence to make and act on one's own decisions, to appreciate the value of reflection and to be effective or try a different approach (QIA, 2008). The Quality Improvement Agency also suggests that, 'to give learners more responsibility for work or learning helps learners to make informed choices and take responsibility for deciding what they need to do in order to learn' (QIA, 2008, p. 1).

In her survey of 80 primary school teachers, Williams (2003) found that teachers held one of two views of the meaning of independence. The first she labelled 'interactionist independence' in which 'children are motivated, good problem solvers, effective communicators and able to seek help as appropriate'; and the second 'isolationist independence', 'where children are trained to develop skills for self-sufficiency and to work alone' (p. 10).

*Are you a believer in interactionists or isolationists?*

Generally, since then, it has become recognized that the 'interactionist' outcome is more appropriate for the promotion of educational goals, particularly creating functional citizens in society. Alexander (2010) in his report on primary schools lists many of the qualities that Williams' survey noted were required of interactionist independent learners. His report summarized these in three aims: 'successful learners', 'confident individuals' and 'responsible citizens' (p. 180).

It is important that children are able to relate to other people and have something positive to contribute. That they learn how to get into a conversation, how to take turns to talk, display what they know or think and generally communicate successfully are all part of an unwritten curriculum (Claxton, 1990). Claxton also says children need to be effective gatherers, organizers, integrators and expressers of knowledge and pupils do this by 'listening, reading, asking questions and discussing'. The QCA (2007) went some way to promoting these broader aims in the Key Stages 3 and 4 National Curriculum (eleven to sixteen years), aims which, unfortunately, have yet to reach the earlier Key Stages.

Williams (2003) offers 15 reasons for children becoming independent. Briefly, these are the promotion of self-esteem, self-motivation, confidence, lessening of attention seeking, resistance to peer pressure, respect for others, ability to take responsibility, good time management, self-discipline, trustworthiness, active learning, satisfaction from personal success, good communication skills, risk taking and the enjoyment of challenge (p. 23).

*How might you promote some of these in your classroom?*

Building on 'confidence', 'reflection' and 'autonomy' (QIA, 2008), what learning environment can we set to promote independent learning? Many of these qualities are already promoted piecemeal in the classroom. Who hasn't used two stars and a wish, talk partners, learners' questions, peer support, reporting back, study skills, pupils' selection of success criteria, assessment for learning and plan-do-review? We recognize these as involving children in their learning but do we see them as strategies to promote independent learning?

*Do we as teachers have a goal of independent learning when we use such strategies?*

What role should the teacher be taking on? Maybe teachers can be too interventionist? Research by Anderson et al. (2003) with 3–5-year-olds found that young children learned a great deal by watching one another, were remarkably focused when allowed to make their own choices, were more likely to say they were stuck if an adult became involved, learned effectively from a competent peer and when issues arose between peers, they were resolved more easily if the adult did not intervene.

*Do we, as teachers, 'take over'?*

To develop children as independent learners is about letting go but only when children have strategies to support themselves. Could it be that multiple actions underpinned by a strong belief and sustained aim to move towards independence for each individual is required? Williams (2003) speaks of a calm, secure atmosphere in a classroom which has 'an ethos which encourages confidence and shared management, has opportunities to contribute, offers open-ended, relevant projects with time to engage and access one's own learning':

> If we value independence, if we are disturbed by the growing conformity of knowledge, of values, of attitudes, which our present system induces, then we may wish to set up conditions, for self-direction, and for self-initiated learning. (Rogers, 1961, p. 292)

*Rogers said this in 1961. Do you think things have changed since then? Are children today encouraged to be more independent or less independent than in the past?*

# References and further reading

Alexander, R. (ed.) (2010) *Children, their World, their Education*, Abingdon: Routledge

Anderson, H., Coltman, P., Page, C. and Whitehead, D. (2003) 'Developing independent learning in children aged 3–5', *European Association for Research on Learning and Instruction Conference Proceedings*, 10th Biennial Conference, Padova, Italy, August 2003

Claxton, G. (1990) *Teaching to Learn: a direction for education*, London: Cassell

QCA (2007) *The National Curriculum for England at Key Stages 3 and 4*, London: QCA

QIA, Quality Improvement Agency (2008) *Teaching and Learning Programme: developing the expert teacher* available at: http://tlp.excellencegateway.org.uk/tlp/xcurricula/el/documents/independence (accessed October 2011)

Rogers, C. (1961) *On Becoming a Person*, Oxford: Houghton-Mifflin

Senior, M. *Ten Practical Ways to make Independent Learning Happen* available at: http://www.seniorpress.co.uk/documents/staffworkshop (accessed October 2011) [contains many practical considerations for promoting independent working in the classroom]

Stevenson, R. and Palmer, J. (1994) *Learning Principles, Process and Practices*, London: Cassell

Teachers' Media (archive of TTRB) *Independent Learners: a classroom approach* available at: http://www.teachersmedia.co.uk (accessed October 2011) [15-minute video of independent learning in a primary school classroom]

Williams, J. (2003) *Promoting Independent Learning in the Primary Classroom*, Buckingham: Open University Press

# Why and how can we engage children with their learning?

## Claire Hewlett

## 5

If we think of learning as being a process of knowledge construction it could be argued that all learning is therefore active in some way. However Watkins (2008) places learning into two distinct categories, what he terms 'learning by doing' and 'learning by sense making'. He argues that it is possible to be physically doing something but for very little learning to be going on. This more passive approach to receiving information may lead to learning being superficial and not always retained.

*We are all familiar with this state of learning. Can you identify times when you have been both a passive learner and an active learner, where you have been meaningfully engaged?*

Active learning recognizes that learning is about constructing meaning. Effective learning requires active engagement and reflection; it involves building knowledge and applying it to new experiences. And, it is often a social activity, involving communicating and working with others. Learning also requires emotional engagement. At times this can be uncomfortable as it can cause self-doubt and anxiety; it is as much about experiencing failure as well as success. We need to be aware that active learning is a highly complex process.

It is Watkins' belief that teachers may be adopting the wrong approach to learning in the classroom, focusing more on the learning by doing rather than by sense making. Rather than focusing on strategies that show children how they can learn, he believes teachers tend to relying on strategies that involve telling children how to be produce better work. Claxton (2007) suggests that we stop saying 'improving learning', which usually is interpreted as improving achievement and instead think about 'expanding learning capacity'. Thinking in this way may help to refocus the mind-set.

*To what extent does your teaching focus on the completion of work rather than how to develop learning skills that can transfer?*

Watkins (2009) uses the metaphor of driving and 'being in the drivers' seat' to represent the learning journey. When driving we have a clear understanding of where we are starting from, where we are going to and how we intend to get there. We make many decisions along the way; some based on prior knowledge, some relating to a new experience. We are confident about applying our understanding of driving to new contexts every day. But Robinson (2006) poses the conundrum: how can we prepare children for a future that we can't grasp? The answer lies in the question itself. We prepare for the unknown by equipping people with the skills and strategies to be able to adapt to change. If we apply the same principles to learning in the classroom then we might be preparing children with the necessary life skills to adapt to change.

There is growing evidence that active learning can improve performance in tests and examinations. One such study, cited by Watkins (2010), involved splitting a group of 15 teachers into two groups. The first group was instructed to help children to learn, the second group to ensure children performed well. Data were collected at various points in the study, including video evidence of the teaching. Results showed teaching in the first group focused more on learners' autonomy while teachers in the second group adopted more controlling strategies focused on instruction. The pupils in the first group performed better overall in the final tests administered as part of the study.

To enable active learning, we need to move away from the concept that it is the teacher who is solely responsible for the learning and be prepared to give some of that responsibility back to the children. Established models of the learning process can provide useful frameworks. Kolb's (1984) seminal study on experiential learning and development produced a holistic learning cycle that is still widely referenced in current learning theory. Though concerned with adult learning development, there is no reason why this cycle cannot be applied with younger learners. Kolb's model identifies four stages of active learning; concrete experience, reflective observation, abstract conceptualization and active experimentation. Table 5.1 illustrates how this approach might look in the primary classroom.

The suggested activities can be used in different ways within the four stages, this is not prescriptive. It is more important to be conscious of how the chosen activities might be supporting different learning processes or stages. Barnes' case studies (2007) on cross-curricular approaches to teaching often show this cycle in action. Using different settings, he shows how it is possible to give children active control of their learning, both emotionally and creatively, and lead their own learning in different

**Table 5.1 Kolb's four active stages of learning**

| Learning stage | What this means | Possible activities |
| --- | --- | --- |
| Concrete experience | Active participation and doing something, rather than passive receipt of information (engagement) | Planning and undertaking a science investigation, problem solving,' hands on' exploration, drawing, active discussion |
| Reflective observation | Reflection on and evaluation of the experience Important to have time for questioning and articulating learning experience with peers and adults (review) | Discussion of results/findings, reflection in plenaries, presentation to others, hot seating, role play |
| Abstract conceptualism | The 'sense-making' stage. Involves further reflection, making comparisons and links to other experiences and what else is known (making sense) | Independent research, problem solving in different contexts, reimagining, presentation of facts, using analogies in role play, debate, thought bubbles |
| Active experimentation | Knowledge transfer. Putting what has been learnt into practice in a different setting or in another way (application) | Provision of planning time, application to real-life contexts or new contexts, publish/exhibit work, unusual subject links in topic work |

Source: adapted from Mobbs, 2003

directions. Watkins et al. (2002) also build on Kolb's model, adding a further complementary cycle promoting learning about learning. This involves how learning can be made an object of 'attention', 'conversation', 'reflection' and 'learning'. This additional framework for planning and reviewing the teaching–learning cycle illustrates how learners might be encouraged to notice different aspects of their learning as they work through each of the four stages. It is extremely useful to consider this model alongside Kolb's original cycle as it provides suggestions for how understanding about learning might be explored confidently through talk.

*Consider a learning experience in your classroom in the light of Kolb's four stages.*

Talk is a key feature of each stage. It is important to get children engaging with metacognitive dialogues (Claxton, 2007; Watkins, 2010) to get them talking about what they are thinking. Using higher ordering questions can challenge children to reflect and articulate their everyday learning. Questions such as:

- How did you do that?
- How did you go about finding out ...?
- How can you teach someone else to do that?
- Did you find out anything you didn't know before?
- If you were the teacher, what would you want to learn next

Teachers need to actively plan for such dialogues to take place. In theory this should not be difficult as we already use a range of strategies that allow for talking and listening. However, we might need to think about how we can utilize reflection time during group work, in plenaries and class discussions much more effectively.

*To what extent do metacognitive dialogues occur with your children? Consider some opportunities for their inclusion.*

Whether or not you agree with Watkins' view of learning, he presents a case that enables us, as teachers, to reflect on our expectations and actions in the classroom. Both he and Robinson look to equipping children for the future and see learning, which can adapt and be sustained, as the way forward.

*What do you think?*

# References and further reading

Barnes, J. (2007) *Cross-Curricular Learning 3–14*, London: Sage

Claxton, G. (2007) 'Expanding young people's capacity to learn', *British Journal of Educational Studies*, 55:2, 115–34

Kolb, D. (1984) *Experiential Learning: experience as the source of learning and development*, 2nd edn, Englewood Cliffs, NJ: Prentice-Hall

Mobbs, R. (2003) *Adult Learning* available at: www.le.ac.uk/users/rjml/etutor Leicester University (accessed October 2011)

Robinson, K. (2006) *Schools Kill Creativity* available at: www.ted.com/talks/ken_robinson says schools kill creativity.html (accessed October 2011)

Watkins, C. (2008) 'Active learning is better learning', *Managing Schools Today*, November/December

—(2009) 'Learners in the driver's seat', *School Leadership Today*, 1:2; available at: www.teachingtimes. com (accessed October 2011)

—(2010) 'Learning, performance and improvement', *Research Matters*, 34, Summer

Watkins, C., Carnell, E., Lodge, C., Wagner, P. and Whalley, C. (2002) *Effective Learning*, NSIN Research Matters, no. 17

# Can we use the built environment to support children's learning?

## Jonathan Barnes

**6**

The 'new science of learning', combining insights from neuroscience, psychology, physiology and sociology, has deepened our understanding of the ways in which we learn. These sciences confirm for example that optimal conditions for learning involve:

- emotional engagement (Damasio and Immordino-Yang, 2007)
- positive mind-sets (Fredrickson, 2009)
- secure environments (Bowlby, 1988)
- social situations (Goswami, 2007)
- complex neural networks covering many areas of the brain (Geake, 2009)
- multisensory and practical activity (Gardner, 1999)
- a genuine desire to find the answers to our questions (Perkins, 2009)
- the development of self-criticality (Robinson and Aronica, 2009).

Involvement in the arts typically provides each of these conditions. The arts are argued powerfully to engage and express the emotions. It is clear that, since time immemorial, dance, painting, drama, storytelling, sung and played music have built and sustained communities and provided personal security and resilience. Modern researchers have demonstrated how creative activity in the arts helps exercise and develop fine sensory distinctions, bolster social cohesion, develop analytical and intuitive modes of learning and nurture personal well-being.

*How far do you go along with this view of the arts? In what way do the arts promote emotional engagement, positive mind-set, social learning and self-criticality?*

The arts are not simply the most ancient forms of human knowledge, they define our present cultures. Built environments physically manifest those cultures. Regardless of home background, we share many material surroundings, yet the buildings we live in and with are rarely the focus of curriculum. Detailed curricular attention to our homes, shops, schools, factories and offices, honours us as individuals and can point towards ways of improving our communities. The enhanced environmental sensitivity that follows often spawns concern for sustainable, more inclusive futures (see Hicks, 2006; Booth and Ainscow, 2011).

*What is your experience of children learning in the local environment? Do you perceive it as honouring?*

The arts offer both personal and communal routes towards understanding our world. While each art has generated its own skills and knowledge, all tend towards wordless communication in their reliance on symbol, feeling and association. Any child's authentic poetic, painted or composed response to inner and outer worlds is an affirmation of both their common humanity and their individuality. Some artistic responses will be influential, others more ordinary, but all involve attempts to make meaning and express a personal or group viewpoint (Craft, 2000).

*Can children have original and valuable ideas in the arts?*

Constructed environments easily become the focus of cross-curricular learning. Buildings may be danced, drawn, photographed, turned into music or become the settings for poetic, descriptive or dramatic writing, but motivation towards such modes of expression may not be automatic. Teachers should therefore consider developing approaches that focus the sensory and emotional attention of learners on places, stimulating interest that will sustain them through the challenges of artistic creation (Barnes, 2008; Barnes, 2011).

*Try some of the focus exercises outlined here and report back (a) on your own engagement, (b) what arts could be involved and (c) the potential for follow-up to extend learning in those arts:*

1  Random words. Fold an A4 sheet into 16 rectangles and unfold it. Each child takes the sheet on a private walk around the chosen area collecting one word for each rectangle as it occurs to them. Tear out the completed 16 rectangles and rearrange them into a poem or meaningful sentence, joining words, definite or indefinite articles or propositions may be added, unwanted words may be left out.

2  Profiles. Explain 'background', 'middle ground' and 'foreground' and set groups of three to draw single unbroken lines to represent the view facing north, south, east and west.

3  Spatialisation. Draw a bird's eye view of your head. Standing still, four children work together to capture the sounds around them by noting the direction of each sound around their drawn head, moving sounds (traffic and aeroplanes)

could be shown by narrowing arrows and accurate descriptions of their changing sounds.

4  Colour chart. Stick double-sided clear tape on a paint swatch showing several different shades of the same colour. Give pairs of children one swatch and ask them to explore their environment sticking on small objects that match the colours of their colour chart.

5  Seeing the join. Use a small viewfinder to isolate the join between two different materials in and around buildings. Carefully draw the join trying to show the different textures and patterns that distinguish each material.

6  Emotional frames. Groups of three children choose and photograph nine contrasting images through a viewfinder labelled with a single emotive word, like beautiful, ugly, dangerous, powerful, sad, happy, green, circular etc.

Through exercises and projects like these the built environment becomes a resource, a treasure trove of fascinating detail. I argue that once children's senses have become engaged and learning has become social and emotionally significant, creative responses are common and genuinely innovative. Through such creativity children learn more deeply and become more caring towards each other and their environment.

# References and further reading

Barnes, J. (2008) 'Music and well-being', *Name Magazine*, 24, Summer, 10–12

—(2011) *Cross-Curricular Learning 3–14*, 2nd edn, London: Sage

Booth, T. and Ainscow, M. (2011) *Index for Inclusion: developing learning and participation in schools*, 2nd edn, Bristol: Centre for Studies on Inclusive Education

Bowlby, J. (1988) *A Secure Base: clinical applications of attachment theory*, London: Routledge

Craft, A. (2000) *Creativity across the Primary Curriculum*, London: Routledge

Damasio, A. and Immordino-Yang, M. (2007) 'We feel therefore we learn: the relevance of affective and social neuroscience to education', *Brain, Mind & Education*, 1:1, 3–10

Fredrickson, B. (2009) *Positivity*, New York: Crown

Gardner, H. (1999) *The Disciplined Mind: what all students should understand*, New York: Simon & Schuster

Geake, J. (2009) *The Brain at School, Educational neuroscience in the classroom*, Maidenhead: Open University Press.

Goswami, U. (2007) 'Children's cognitive development & learning', *Primary Review Research Briefings* 2/1, Cambridge: University of Cambridge Faculty of Education

Hicks, D. (2006) *Lessons for the Future: the missing dimension in education*, London: Routledge

Panksepp, J. (1998) *Affective Neuroscience: the origins of animal & human emotions*, New York: Oxford University Press

Perkins, D. (2009) *Making Learning Whole: how seven principles of teaching can transform education*, San Francisco: Jossey-Bass

Robinson, K. and Aronica, L. (2009) *The Element: how finding your passion changes everything*, London: Allen Lane

[*Note*: Visit English Heritage and the Commission for Architecture and the Built Environment's 'Engaging Places' website for ideas, plans, places and resources to help you plan arts activities in the built environment. http://www.engagingplaces.org.uk/home.]

# What do we understand from using images in the classroom?

## Peter Dorman

**7**

Geoffrey Mallin and John McDowell's film of the Battle of the Somme, which is available on the Imperial War Museum (IWM) site, demonstrates the complexity of using images uncritically. One extract that has been shown many times on television purports to show troops 'going over the top' and attacking into no-mans' land. It has become an almost defining image. We see the men drawn up in battle formation. They climb the parapet and move out into the fog. One even falls dead. Yet this particular sequence was, in fact, staged well away from the actual battle. The reason for this was simple and driven by the large, heavy and vulnerable camera technology available at the time. The episode can be perhaps seen as a re-creation of real events but not a strict recording of real events. But does this make it any less real? Is, for example, the opening sequence of *Saving Private Ryan* 'real' in the sense that a strict documentary records the actuality of historical events? And, because we *can* stage events, does this mean that all film and video footage *are* staged. Did, for example, Neil Armstrong step onto the Moon in 1969 and the Twin Towers collapse on 9/11 or are these, as conspiracy theorists assert, simply staged events? We talk about the use of *scientific method* as a means of trying to ensure that researchers seek for objective truth; is it possible to ensure a similar 'visual truth' when using images?

*Consider one of your memorable images. How selective and stereotypical is it?*

Related, but often more subtle, problems lie when using any form of visual resource in the classroom. As Scoffham (2006) notes, in Unit 10 of the QCA geography schemes of work, *A Village in India*, readers need to be 'aware of bias and stereotypical images which can sometimes be found in locality packs'. Their uncritical or uninformed use can lead the unwary into the trap of assuming that images simply capture the total reality of a situation rather than being a particular selection and a representation which has been constructed by an author. As professional educators we always need to be wary of their intended and unintended motives.

*What images have used with children and what messages are they conveying?*

Before visiting a school in India recently, I worked with some Year 4 children in a local primary school. They had just completed a term's work on life in India in which they had used many resources including the internet. One website they had visited showed pictures of life in the area of southern India that I was to visit. The images showed life in a rural community on the banks of a meandering river. People were shown living on large rice boats with men fishing with Chinese-style nets. I asked the children what kinds of question they might like me to try to find answers to. The list included: 'Do you have many children in your school?' 'Do you wear school uniforms?' 'How big is your family?' 'Do you have a father and if so what work does he do?' 'What sacred animals do you have?' 'Do you have clean water?' 'What sport do you like?'

After the visit I could report back to the children that the school had 2500 pupils. The average family size of the class I worked in was two. About 90% of the pupils' fathers worked in Dubai in order to send money home for their families. The children wore differently coloured uniforms each day depending on the day of the week. Most were Christian and had lots of pet animals, mainly birds. As for their favourite sport, the answer was a universal 'Cricket!' As for the rice boats, well they certainly are there but now the only people who use them are the tourists who flock to the area from inside and outside India. And the fishing nets? I took a photograph that was almost identical to that on the website but then I turned a little to the left and photographed the 400 or more trawlers of the Keralan fishing fleet next to them. The images that the children had seen and had assumed to 'be' India were as true as pictures of Morris dancers, Beefeaters or red double-decker buses provide a complete representation of England.

*Is there a place for stereotypical images in school or should we show a range of images expressing similarity as well as difference?*

Images involve a relationship between the image maker, the image as an object, the subject of the image (the referent) and the viewer's interpretation and response to what is seen. Wright, (1999, cited in Banks, 2001) suggests that this set of relationships underpins the possible 'multiple narratives', what he terms the 'multivocality' of images. He further suggests that images should be interpreted in three ways: by *looking at*, by *looking through* and by 'looking behind' the image. Applying this analysis to photographs: they can be *looked at* as objects that can be understood in purely technical terms of focus, colour saturation, depth of field, lighting. Using such criteria we can judge whether a photograph is 'good' or 'bad'. When we 'look through' the image we react to the actual content. We respond differently for example to photographs of people if they are friends or relatives or loved ones than if they are simply an unnamed person with which we have no connection. For this reason, we treasure photographs that may not be good in technical terms, but remind us of people we know or particular times and places in lives. When we *look through* the photograph we start to bring a range of cultural and ethical judgments to bear on the image.

*What images do you choose to convey in different contexts and why?*

*Think for example of the image that people present of themselves on their personal Facebook pages; is this the same image they the wish to present publicly to say a future employer?*

*Why are people often told to face the camera and smile when their photograph is taken? Is the resulting photograph a record of a specific time and place or is it more a way of creating a future memory, an image that will allow us to look back at our past and remember how happy we were when it was taken?*

Remember, that whenever we use any visual resource what we are presenting is always an incomplete and partial view. As professionals we have at all times to avoid the 'zoo mentality', which exoticises difference and in so doing underpins inadequate and uncritical practice. Effective teaching challenges rather than reinforces stereotypes.

# References and further reading

Banks, M. (2001) *Visual Methods in Social Research*, London: Sage

Pink, S. (2002) *Doing Visual Ethnography*, London: Sage

Pinney, C. (1997) *Camera Indica: the social life of Indian photographs*, London: Reakton Books.

Qualifications and Curriculum Authority (QCA) (1998) *Geography Unit 10. A Village in India*, London: QCA

Scoffham, S. (2006) 'Problems with distant places' presented to the *Conference in Primary Geography Education Research*, Charney Manor, Charney Bassett, Oxfordshire, 23–25 February 2007

Sontag, S. (1997) *On Photography*, 3rd edn, London: Penguin Books

Wright, T. (1999) *The Photography Handbook*, London: Routledge

[*Note*: The Battle of the Somme film sequence is available online at: http://collections.iwm.org.uk/server.php?show=ConWebDoc.3802&navId=157   Or search for 'The Battle of the Somme Imperial War Museum'.]

# 8 Do displays contribute to children's learning?

Bridie Price

---

Displays may be used for a number of purposes that could include: a celebration of children's work and efforts; a stimulus for learning; to provide information; or they might be used to create an aesthetically pleasing environment in which children work. For a visitor or parent an initial impression of a school can be created by its displays.

*Do some or all of these purposes contribute to children's learning and how could they do this?*

For a number of teachers, displays are an opportunity to celebrate pupils' work and to show children, parents, governors and other visitors to the school that they value their work and efforts. Displaying children's own work can encourage them to take pride in it and lead to greater motivation (Muijs and Reynolds, 2005). These displays could also help to promote a child's self-esteem and thereby help develop a positive impact on learning (Kershner and Pointon, 2000). However, if a child's work is not included in the display this could have a negative effect on them that may alienate or demotivate them. Other children might want to take their work home so may not want their work on display.

*How do you balance the need for inclusion with the maintenance of quality?*

Some teachers question the impact such displays have on children's learning (Smith and Call, 1999). They suggest that although this may be an important aspect for early years' classrooms so that children feel a sense of belonging and security, those who feel valued through other means do not require such affirmation. Others argue that displays are a distraction.

*Do you agree with Smith and Call? Should the use of display decline as children get older?*

Displays that arouse a child's curiosity and are thought provoking can provide a stimulus for learning (Clegg and Billington, 2002). These displays could include collections of objects for children to explore, pictures to observe closely and respond to accompanying questions, investigations or problems to solve. But how do children engage with these displays and are children given the opportunity to engage with them formally or informally? If such opportunities are not offered what message does this convey to children about the importance and value of the displays?

*What use do you make of interactive displays and what contribution do they make to children's learning?*

Support for children's learning is often presented through the use of informative displays. For example, a word display could be used to support or extend writing or another could include key facts, e.g. numbers, colours, shapes and so on. In research by Kershner and Pointon (2000), several children mentioned that although some displays provided relevant information and helped with their learning, others did not. In some instances, they were unsure about a display's purpose as its intention had not been explained to them. Even though displays may be used to offer support for children's learning could they become reliant on this support and not move to a more independent approach to their learning?

Working walls, as recommended by the Department for Education and Skills (DES) (2006) provide support for current learning in literacy and numeracy (although some teachers have applied a similar approach across other areas of the curriculum). Such walls display the learning outcomes, success criteria and offer some modelled examples, including models of learning processes and learning steps. They incorporate exemplifications of curricular targets so that children can see how their learning towards this is developed. Opportunities are also provided for children's contributions. The DES suggests that by using this approach children will know what they are learning and how this learning process develops over a period of time.

*What is your experience of children's engagement with this type of display and their effectiveness?*

A number of school display policies actively encourage the involvement of pupils in the decision making and preparation of displays. Hegarty (1996) argues that by providing an opportunity for children to engage with the planning and creation of displays children's skills in design, planning and collaboration can be developed. This involvement would also provide scope for the concepts, skills and content knowledge of the curriculum to be discussed and communicated by the children.

*Will active engagement by children in planning displays help to provide a more meaningful learning resource and what impact might this have on their learning?*

It does not necessarily follow that a display falls neatly into one or other of the categories mentioned here. Some displays may have a number of purposes. A display intended to celebrate and value children's work could serve this purpose and also be aesthetically pleasing. This could have a positive impact on a child's self-esteem and motivation. It may also serve to set expectations for the quality of work and effort required and so act to raise standards in learning for others in the class. A display celebrating all the school's work during a themed week, e.g. art week or mathematics week, could also demonstrate progression in this particular subject.

There are a number of reasons for creating and maintaining displays but how do we know whether children use these to support or develop their learning? In some of the examples just mentioned, the proof may be evident in the child's work or responses. Displays could encourage physical interaction on the part of the children so that they use aspects of the display to explore or physically manipulate something, e.g. connecting different materials in an electric circuit display to test for conductivity. In this way, teachers will be able to gauge, to some extent, whether the display contributes to learning.

*Is it possible for teachers to integrate this form of assessment into their busy schedule?*

Individual participants in classrooms may have different perceptions about the purpose of display. One might also challenge the teacher as to the purpose of them. If it is intended to facilitate children's learning, how do we, as teachers, ensure that all children and individuals in the classroom are aware of its purpose and that the display is not just wallpaper or a distraction?

# References and further reading

Ceppi, G. and Zini, M. (eds) (1998) *Children, Spaces, Relations: meta-project for an environment for young children*, Reggio Emilia, Italy: Reggio Children

Clegg, D. and Billington, S. (2002) 'Classroom layout, resources and display', in Pollard, A. (ed.) *Readings for Reflective Teaching*, London: Continuum

Department for Education and Skills (2006) *The Learning Environment as a Tool for Learning* available at: http://www.teachfind.com/national-strategies/whole-school-cpd-improve-learning-and-teaching (accessed August 2011)

Hegarty, P. (1996) 'Quality on display: tasks, learning and the classroom', in Cooper, H., Hegarty, P., Hegarty, P. and Simco, N. (1996) *Display in the Classroom*, London: David Fulton

Kershner, R. and Pointon, P. (2000) 'Children's views of the primary classroom as an environment for work and learning', *Research in Education*, 64, 64–77

Muijs, D. and Reynolds, D. (2005) *Effective Teaching*, London: Sage

Ramsey, J. and Fowler, M. (2004) 'What do you notice? Using posters containing questions and general instructions to guide preschoolers' science and mathematics learning', *Early Child Development and Care*, 174:1, 31–45

Smith, A. and Call, N. (1999) *The ALPS Approach*, Stafford: Network Educational Press Ltd

Tarr, P. (2004) 'Consider the walls', *Young Children*, 59:3, 88–92; available at http://journal.naeyc.org/btj/200405 (accessed August 2011)

Teachers TV (2006) *Positive Learning Environments – primary* available at http://www.teachersmedia.co.uk/videos/positive-learning-environment-primary (accessed August 2011)

# Do interactive whiteboards support or reduce creativity in the classroom?

**9**

Karl Bentley

The interactive whiteboard (IWB) has become a standard fixture in the majority of primary school classrooms. Indeed, classroom layout has been subtly altered so as to make the IWB a central feature. Connected to a computer, the internet, speakers and, more recently, digital visualizers, there is no doubt that the IWB has developed into a potentially powerful technological device. However, the question that must be asked is, do interactive whiteboards support or reduce creativity in the classroom?

*Consider the following two scenarios and discuss how the teacher has used the IWB to support children's learning and in particular support their creativity and why this may have occurred? Can you suggest further ways use of the IWB could be developed?*

Scenario 1: In the first classroom, only the very basic features of the IWB are utilized and there is minimal or often no interaction with the board by the learners in the classroom. Usage remains similar to that of the 'wipe board', which remains in frequent use. There are many paper notes and bits of information posted around the edge of the interactive board.

Scenario 2: In the second classroom, the IWB is used in conjunction with the internet to provide visual, kinaesthetic and auditory resources. Often these are annotated before or during the lesson. The teacher uses the board with occasional contributions from the children but always under supervision.

The second teacher may seem at first to be fully utilizing the IWB, but as Mercer et al. (2010) state: 'One should not judge teachers' uses of the IWB by how "whizzy" they are; we should judge them by how well they harness the technology to serve effective pedagogic strategies' (p. 203). It also raises the question of pupil participation.

*Consider a lesson in which you used the IWB. Why did you decide this was the best way to teach this objective?*

If we want to enhance the teaching and learning in the classroom, we must take heed of research that indicates that teachers change their practice in ICT more easily when change is accompanied by organizational support (Davis et al., 2009).

*What support is available in your school or from outside?*

A key point to note in research carried out by Mercer et al. (2010) is that the board itself doesn't create any more interaction in a classroom. Rather it is the ability of the teacher to exploit the potential interactivity of the board that makes all the difference. Best results are achieved when the teacher, the learners and the other adults in the classroom are all using the full complement of resources available from an IWB. Also when the whole class or groups or individuals are interacting with the IWB as and when the teacher deems it most effective; when the adult support is fully at home with the IWB and happily uses it to meet the learning objectives planned and agreed on with the class teacher.

Consider the following issues in relation to your classroom:

- Where is the space for spontaneity and in turn creativity to develop? Compton (2007) states, 'the philosophy and documentation currently in place in schools, allows teachers the freedom to give greater responsibility to children of all ages, developing their creativity as well as their learning' (p. 115).
- Has the IWB made the teaching so easy that the learning has begun to suffer? Smith et al. (2006, p. 455) refer to this as being 'seduced by the technology'.
- Are the children and teaching assistants involved in the planning of the use of the IWB? Can the children and adult support question what the best resources would be, including the use of the IWB?
- Is there flexibility built into lessons to allow for deviations from the plans?
- Does the class accept and understand that some children find resources other than the IWB may suit their learning styles more effectively?
- Is the visualizer, attached to the IWB, utilized for peer review of work and recording of assessments, as well as using other recording strategies?
- Is the IWB used as a resource and a support for learning without directing it? Can the children choose to use it?
- Are all the learners taught to assess the purposefulness of the IWB and its associated devices and accept their strengths and weaknesses?

Some of these approaches are not used in the classroom because children need time and support to be discriminatory about their choice and use of resources such as an IWB. Ultimately, everyone should regard the IWB as a liberating and enabling tool that allows them to co-construct new understanding of both subject content and pedagogy in the primary classroom.

# References and further reading

Beauchamp, G. (2004) 'Teacher use of the interactive whiteboard (IWB) in primary schools – towards an effective transition framework', *Technology, Pedagogy and Education*, 13:3, 327–48

Compton, A. (2007) 'What does creativity mean in English education?', *Education 3–13*, 35:2, 109–16

Davis, N., Preston, C. and Sahin, I. (2009) 'ICT teacher training: evidence for multilevel evaluation from a national initiative', *British Journal of Educational Technology*, 40:1, 135–48

Mercer, N., Hennessy, S. and Warwick, P. (2010) 'Using interactive whiteboards to orchestrate classroom dialogue', *Technology, Pedagogy and Education*, 19:2, 195–209

Smith, F., Hardman, F. and Higgins, S. (2006) 'The impact of interactive whiteboards on teacher–pupil interaction in the National Literacy and Numeracy Strategies', *British Educational Research Journal*, 32:3, 443–57

Wood, R. and Ashfield, J. (2008) 'The use of the interactive whiteboard for creative teaching and learning in literacy and mathematics: a case study', *British ournal of Educational Technology*, 39:1, 84–96

[Both major interactive whiteboard manufacturers provide extensive support and access to learning resources and research: Promethean: http://www.prometheanplanet.com/en-gb/; Smart Boards: http://www.smarttech.com/gb/Solutions/Education+Solutions.]

# Is learning outside the classroom worth it?

## Michael Green

## 10

Over the last decade, there have been considerable developments to promote out-of-classroom education, examples of which include the launch of the Learning Outside the Classroom Manifesto, the creation of a quality badge for providers of learning outside the classroom and a significant investment by the Department for Education and Skills (DfES, 2006) in the Council for Learning Outside the Classroom. Such developments reflect the previous government's and others' strong beliefs in not only the broad range of benefits associated with learning outside the classroom, but also the growing concerns about the marked decline in the opportunities being afforded to children to learn outside the classroom (Rickinson et al., 2004; Bilton, 2010).

*What opportunities have you had for working outside the classroom with your class and what do you perceive as the difficulties?*

While it is difficult to quantify the amount of outdoor learning that does take place every year some studies have been undertaken to illustrate the problem. Such a decline, for example, was aptly illustrated by the Forest Stewardship Council in 2004 where they identified a 30-year decline in the number of secondary students using their facilities in the United Kingdom. It is acknowledged that the decline in opportunities is most acute in secondary education, however, the decline is also evident in the primary sector (NFER, 2004). The reasons for this are well documented (for example, Peacock, 2006; Malone, 2008; Bilton, 2010; Sangster and Green, 2010; Waite, 2011) and have been attributed to a number of key issues including: the perceived concerns regarding health and safety (not helped by adverse media headlines), lack of teacher confidence in relation to skills and knowledge, pressures of the curriculum and the school timetable and, finally, bureaucratic demands on teachers. Given such daunting obstacles, the question that has to be asked is why is such provision receiving so much positive attention and support from all quarters, including government level and what does research tell us about the contribution that outdoor learning can have on children?

*What do you think are the benefits to children of working away from the classroom?*

Before I go on to attempt to answer such 'big' questions, I think it's important first to consider what one actually means when referring to 'learning outside the classroom'. Malone (2008, p. 7) provides a very clear definition of learning outside the classroom as 'any' opportunity initiated by teachers and/or students to engage with alternative learning settings to complement and/or supplement the formal indoors classroom curricula. The range of alternative learning settings that exist are considerable and include: museums, libraries, outdoor and adventure settings, zoos, art galleries, the school grounds, urban spaces etc.

According to Gould (2003) it is essential that teachers 'appreciate the power' of providing children with opportunities to learn outside the classroom. Historically, the argument for providing children with this type of learning experience has been based on an 'assumption' that it is beneficial (Malone, 2008, p. 7). There is no question, however, that, in recent years, the importance of providing opportunities for children to learn outside the classroom has become the subject of considerable research (e.g. Rickinson, 2001; Dillon et al., 2005; Peacock, 2006; Malone, 2008; Green, 2011). Such research has yielded a number of key areas in which children benefit from engaging in such outdoor learning opportunities. What follows is an introduction to the key findings in relation to two areas of research: the link between children's emotional responses to learning outside the classroom and its contribution towards learning and the impact of learning outside the classroom on children's levels of motivation. It's important to acknowledge at this stage, however, that there are many more benefits such as physical benefits and social benefits to name but two.

The opening paragraph of the Learning Outside the Classroom Manifesto suggests that out of classroom learning experiences are:

> the most memorable learning experiences, helping us to make sense of the world around us by making links between feelings and learning [...] They allow us to transfer learning experienced outside to the classroom and vice versa. (DfES, 2006, p. 3)

If we consider then the role of feelings and emotions in learning then one could argue that there is a clear link between learning outside the classroom and cognitive development. Scoffham and Barnes (2010) make a very compelling case for the role of emotions in learning, in particular how the feeling of happiness can impact on children's lives and their learning. They draw on the work of Panksepp (1998) who discusses how the presence of chemicals such as dopamine during emotional responses can 'instigate behaviour'. He points out that 'when dopamine synapses are active in abundance, a person feels as if he or she can do anything'. Such a feeling, Bredecamp et al. (1992) would argue, 'fosters a love of learning, curiosity, attention and self-direction' (ibid., 1992, p. 3). There is a substantial amount of literature concerning how learning outside the classroom provides 'good memories' (for example, Elliot and Davis, 2004). It is often the case that most of us are able to recall positive memories from our childhood linked to school trips. It is suggested by Carver (2003) that these memories are 'good' and long lasting as they are related to positive emotions linked to the experience.

Teachers at both primary and secondary level value out-of-classroom learning settings for their ability to increase levels of motivation and interest towards different subject areas. Studies that have also sought to gain the views of children in relation to learning outside the classroom overwhelmingly comment on children's positive attitudes about the experience (Malone, 2008). As Bredecamp et al. (1992) note: '[A]ctivities that are based on children's interests provide a motivation for learning.' Nixon et al. (1996) argue that learning actually depends on motivation and they go on to suggest that traditional teaching and learning methods, as seen in many of our primary schools, only bring about apathy towards learning, decrease motivation and the standards agenda can create anxiety instead of joy. This view is echoed too by Galton (2007) who warns that in our current primary education: '[M]otivation appears to have changed in ways that do not encourage pupils to take up new challenges or express themselves creatively' (p. 28).

In contrast, according to Peacock (2006, p. 5) learning outside the classroom has the potential to enable children to 'develop positive attitudes, arouse learners' interests and improve behaviour'. The significance of this is highlighted by Barnes (2007, p. 115) who state that developing a positive attitude can 'result in a strong sense of "self-efficacy", the ability to persuade oneself that one is able to reach a particular goal or set of goals'. It seems therefore that learning outside the classroom has a key role to play in learning and every opportunity for children to engage in such experiences should be fully exploited by teachers. Braund and Reiss (2004) define learning to be 'what people do when they want to make sense of the world' (ibid., 2004, p. 5). In other words, learning does not occur unless people want to make sense of something. One could argue then that curiosity can be a driver for exploration that can lead to children discovering new things for themselves. They go on to argue that:

> [When] pupils visit or are taught in places that explain science in new and exciting ways, they frequently seem to be more enthused. There is, we believe, something about these contexts and places that brings about change through increasing the desire in people to find out and understand more. (p. 5)

*How effective have you found learning outside the classroom to be?*

It seems, therefore that learning outside the classroom is crucial to creating motivation, which is integral to children's cognitive development. However, it is important to acknowledge that there are limitations to such benefits. Rickinson et al. (2004) note that poor out-of-classroom experiences are often the result of a lack of planning and follow-up activities and can result in poor learning.

To summarize: if, as Noddings (2003) asserts, 'education should contribute significantly to personal and collective happiness' (ibid., 2003, p. 1) then one can easily see the case for learning outside the classroom being strengthened in the primary context. It is, therefore, essential that as educators we harness the potential that such opportunities can yield.

# References and further reading

Beames, S., Higgins, P. and Nicol, R. (2011) *Learning Outside the Classroom: theory and guidelines for practice*, London: Routledge

Bilton, H. (2010) *Outdoor Learning in the Early Years*, Abingdon: Routledge

Braund, M. and Reiss, M. (eds) (2004) 'The nature of learning science outside the classroom', *Learning Science Outside the Classroom*, London: Routledge Falmer

BredeKamp, S., Knuth, R., Kuresh, L. and Shulman, D. (1992) *What Does Research Say about Early Childhood Education?* available at: http://eclkc.ohs.acf.hhs.gov/ hslc/tta-system/teaching/eecd/ Curriculum/ Planning/edudev_art_ 00421_081806.html (accessed March 2011)

Carver, C. (2003) 'Pleasure as a sign you can attend to something else: placing positive feelings within a general model of affect', *Cognition and Emotions*, 17:2, 241–61

Department for Education and Skills (DfES) (2006) *Learning Outside the Classroom Manifesto*, London: DfES

Dillon, J., Morris, M., O'Donnell, L., Rickinson, M. and Scott, W. (2005) *Engaging and Learning with the Outdoors*, Bath: CREE.

Elliot, S. and Davis, J. (2004) 'Mud pies and daisy chains: connecting young children and nature', *Every Child*, 10:4, 4–5

Galton, M. (2007) *Learning and Teaching in the Primary Classroom*, London: Sage

Gould, H. (2003) *Settings Other than Schools: initial teacher training placements in museums, libraries and archives*, York: Yorkshire Museums, Library and Archives Council (YMLAC)

Green, M. (2011) *An Exploration of the Lived Experiences of Year Six Children on a Residential Trip to Normandy*, unpublished MA thesis, Canterbury Christ Church University

Malone, K. (2008) *Every Experience Matters*, Leicester: Farming and Countryside Education

National Foundation for Education Research (NfER) (2004) *Education Outside the Classroom: research to identify what training is offered by initial teacher training institutions*, London: DfES

Nixon, J., Martin, J., McKeown, P. and Ranson, S. (1996) *Encouraging Learning*, Buckingham: Open University Press

Noddings, N. (2003) *Happiness and Education*, Cambridge: Cambridge University Press

Panksepp, J. (1998) *Affective Neuroscience: the foundations of human and animal emotion*, Oxford: Oxford University Press

Peacock, A. (2006) *Changing Minds: the lasting impact of school trips*, Exeter: University of Exeter

Rickinson, M. (2001) 'Learners and learning in environmental education: a critical review of the evidence', *Environmental Education Research*, 7:3, 207–320

Rickinson, M., Dillon, J., Teamey, K., Morris, M., Choi, M., Sanders, D. and Benefield, P. (2004) *A Review of Research on Outdoor Learning*, Shrewsbury: Field Studies Council

Sangster, M. and Green, M. (2010) 'The value of an alternative placement for student teachers in initial teacher education', paper presented at the *European Education Research Conference*, Helsinki, 25–27 September. Available at http://www.eera-ecer.eu/ecer-programmes/conference/ecer-2010/contribution/730-2/?no_cache=1&cHash=21044039e2 (accessed October 2010)

Scoffham, S. and Barnes, J. (2010) *Happiness Matters: towards a pedagogy of happiness and well-being*, unpublished article, Canterbury: Canterbury Christ Church University

Trant, J. (2010) *The Essential Guide to Successful School Trips*, Harlow: Pearson Education

Waite, S. (2011) *Children Learning Outside the Classroom from Birth to Eleven*, London: Sage

# 11 What is the value of encouraging talk in your classroom?

Jill Matthews

Did you know that experienced beekeepers can tell by listening to the buzz how contented their bees are; whether they have enough sources of nectar and pollen, whether they are about to swarm or whether they are under stress? The health of the hive, its productivity and its potential for survival depends on the queen bee. Using this analogy, the class teacher orchestrates the harmony of active learning within a primary classroom. A good classroom 'buzz' or discourse depends on a quality learning environment. Pupil–pupil discourse arises from a good classroom ethos created by the actions of the teacher, the way the teacher organizes the class and the nature of the tasks provided. These actions will, in turn, influence the level of engagement of the learners.

*What different levels of 'buzz' have you noticed in your class? What role do the teacher and other adults play in promoting discussion? How might your answers to the questions affect the quality of the talk within the classroom?*

Over the past decade in England, official guidance in the National Literacy and National Numeracy Strategies (NLS, NNS) superseded by the Primary Framework has emphasized the importance of whole-class teaching. In a climate that values 'achieving standards, base target levels, and test performance', pacey, teacher-directed, instructional lessons might appear superficially 'outstanding' and meet expectations for 'interactive teaching'. However, further, deeper exploration of the learning taking place within the lesson might reveal a different story. Is there good interaction? Do all children participate? Who is doing the talking? One might need to reconsider what is meant by 'interactive'.

Findings emerging from the ESRC project (Burns and Myhill, 2004) suggested that teachers still dominate the talk within classrooms. The researchers found that the patterns of dialogue were still variations of the Sinclair-Coulthard (1975) model of 'initiation–response–feedback'. The most common form of question required a factual answer and the most common function was elicitation. The problem with this approach is that, as Wood

(1988) suggests, it favours the children who know the answers already and alienates the children who do not. It does not give the children a chance to explore the question being asked. Possible ambiguities in children's understanding the purpose of a question were highlighted in Donaldson's (1987) re-evaluation of Piaget's developmental stages. Such questioning models do not encourage children to discuss ideas at their own level, in their own words or engage with a range of possible explorative responses that Mercer and Littleton (2007) describe as exploratory talk.

*In your experience, to what extent does whole class teaching allow for deep individual engagement? What learning is taking place in this organizational model?*

This is not to suggest that there is no place for teacher–pupil dialogue. It is more a question of the *quality* of the interaction and the degree to which the learner has the opportunity to articulate their thinking (Alexander, 2001, 2004). The role of the teacher should be less that of interrogator and more of facilitator. This approach is reflected in assessment for learning strategies (Black et al., 2003) and the concept of the teacher as supporter of the learner's emerging understanding; a role that prompts and encourages the child to elaborate and explain their understanding.

In a sociocultural approach to teaching and learning, children are required to co-construct new conceptual understanding with others; using language to test out their ideas and to articulate the truth as they perceive it (Mercer and Littleton, 2007). Most children acquire language and use it to communicate successfully within the home, with other children and the significant adults in their lives (Wells, 2009). In the home, this usually occurs in 1:1 dyadic exchanges. In a busy classroom, opportunities for dyadic exchanges with an adult are relatively rare. Children also have to develop the skills to be able to function effectively within a group. This includes learning to listen attentively to others, waiting for a turn to speak, being able to frame questions appropriately.

To enable these group work skills to develop how might the teacher physically organize the classroom?

*Consider the organization of your classroom and ask yourself how these organizational strategies affect a child's ability to function effectively within a group and promote discussion?*

- Are the desks in rows or groups?
- Do the desks always stay in the same position?
- Do the children sit in the same place throughout the lesson/week/year?

- Do the children work alone or in pairs during the whole class input? (Talk partners.)
- Do the children always work with the same children?
- Are the children seated boy/girl/boy/girl?
- Are discussions between pupils given any time or value? (e.g. reporting back after a task).

Attention is rarely given to the potential for group collaborative learning (Burns and Myhill, 2004). Kutnick and Berdonini (2009) indicate the interventions undertaken in the SPRinG project successfully demonstrate that young children can, already at the ages of five and six, become productive, collaborative, mutually supportive learners. The teachers involved on the project modelled and supported the children's working together as a group on a range of tasks that required collaboration or cooperation. This relational training was not tied to a specific area of the curriculum. Classrooms were adapted to enable the children to engage in the group work as independently as possible. The project's findings suggested that learning to relate productively within the group affected children's attainment in a positive way.

Focusing on pupil–pupil dialogue in the same project, Baines et al. (2009) found that the SPRinG pupils' group work involved more explicit reasoning discussions and children were able to infer beyond the information provided for the task. The quality of the 'talk' was at a higher cognitive level than that of the control groups. Baines et al. (ibid.) also found that the SPRinG groups were able to sustain focus for longer periods. The findings of the SPRinG research indicates that the teacher's role is:

- to organize opportunities for learning which provoke a degree of cognitive conflict and appropriate challenge; where the outcome is not certain so that children want to engage and talk about their ideas
- to promote an inclusive collaborative learning environment where all are encouraged to contribute actively.

Claxton (2007) recommends that teachers help children to build 'learning muscles', which prepare them for learning in a world that is unpredictable and where they need to have the courage and tenacity to find out the answers. Claxton (2006) highlights the importance of developing the soft key skills such as communication, collaboration, an ability to solve problems and think outside the box. He believes that children need to be active learners, self-regulating and learn to operate with increasing independence of the teacher and supporting adults.

*Do you agree with Guy Claxton's view of learning?*

Learning in school is different from learning on a 1:1 basis with a parent or at an out-of-school club. But the children's level of engagement with their learning should be similar to be successful. Significant, creative and imaginative learning experiences are essential if children are to be motivated to engage in learning. The teacher's role should be to entice the child into an irresistible puzzle to be solved, a story that has to be finished, the need to find an explanation. Teaching should be more than the transmission of facts and practice of skills. Skills and competencies must be developed but learning has to be relevant, real and risky. How is this best achieved? Often this is achieved through the use of meaningful and purposeful contexts. Children who are actively engaged in their learning engage in meaningful 'talk'. They share ideas, test theories, try things out with their peers. They enjoy and participate constructively and collaboratively in the learning activity. There is a contented hum of purposeful conversation.

*When is the 'buzz' best in your classroom?*

# References and further reading

Alexander, R. (2001) *Culture and Pedagogy: international comparisons in primary education*, Oxford: Blackwell

—(2004) *Towards Dialogic Teaching*, Thirsk: Dialogos UK Ltd

Baines, E., Rubie-Davies, C. and Blatchford, P. (2009) 'Improving pupil group work interaction and dialogue in primary classrooms: results from a year-long intervention study', *Cambridge Journal of Education*, 39:1, 95–117

Black, P., Harrison, C., Lee, C., Marshall, B. and Wiliam, D. (2003) *Assessment for Learning: putting it into practice*, Maidenhead: Open University Press

Burns, C. and Myhill, D. (2004) 'Interactive or inactive? A consideration of the nature of interaction in whole class teaching', *Cambridge Journal of Education*, 34:1, 35–49

Claxton, G. (2006) 'Thinking at the edge: developing soft creativity', *Cambridge Journal of Education*, 36:3, 351–62

—(2007) 'Expanding young people's capacity to learn', *British Journal of Educational Studies*, 55:2, 115–34

Donaldson, M. (1987) *Children's Minds*, London: Fontana Press

Haworth, A. (2001) 'The repositioning of oracy: a millennium project?', *Cambridge Journal of Education*, 31:1, 11–23

Kutnick, P. and Berdonini, L. (2009) 'Can the enhancement of group working in classrooms provide a basis for effective communication in support of school-based cognitive achievement in classrooms of young learners?', *Cambridge Journal of Education*, 39:1, 71–94

Mercer, N. and Littleton, K. (2007) *Dialogue and the Development of Children's Thinking, A Sociocultural Approach*, Abingdon: Routledge

Sinclair, J. and Coulthard, R. (1975) *Towards an Analysis of Discourse: the English used by teachers and pupils*, Oxford: Oxford University Press

Wells, G. (2009) *The Meaning Makers: learning to talk and talking to learn*, 2nd edn, Bristol: Multilingual Matters

Wood, D. (1988) *How Children Think & Learn: the social contexts for cognitive development*, Oxford: Blackwell

# Does rewarding children lead to independent learners?

## Margaret Sangster

## 12

It is a generally held belief that teachers wish to encourage children to become independent in their learning. This belief is probably underpinned by the hope that all children will be able to eventually manage their own learning and will become productive and self-motivating members of society. They may find themselves in a job where they have to follow orders and money is the reward, but there will be more to their lives than this. They will need to make decisions, initiate and engage for the sake of engagement. Self-motivation and decision making are two key factors in operating independently.

For some children any motivation to learn is an issue, let alone self-motivation. Maslow (1943) is famous for his hierarchy of motivation in which he claimed it was difficult for students to be creative, solve problems and meet challenge if other needs were not met first. He proposed that fundamental needs begin with physical needs such as food, health and sleep, followed by a safe and secure environment. Above this he placed a need to belong socially, be accepted by the group and be successful. If all these are in place, self-esteem can be responded to through status, responsibility, confidence and respect. And then children can respond to creativity and challenge.

*Consider children in your class. Where are they on Maslow's hierarchy and can schools and teachers make provision for any of these needs?*

Lack of motivation to learn was one of the drivers of Black and Wiliam's research *Inside the Black Box* (1998). They were tasked with how to engage disaffected secondary students in learning. By close observation over a number of years they found that by using certain teaching strategies, students would become better engaged in learning. These are strategies that you could use as a teacher and some of them will be established procedures in your school already. For example, you may already create time to respond to feedback, require greater participation by pupils, get children involved in self-assessment and use good questioning techniques.

A commonly used strategy in primary schools used to motivate children is a reward system. House points, golden time, stars, marbles in the jar, smiley faces, ticks and comments such as 'well done' and 'good work' are all forms of reward, given out by the teacher. They are used to reward good work or good behaviour or effort or even for a task accomplished. All are extrinsic rewards as they are provided by someone else. A scientific interpretation would be to say they are instruments of behaviour modification in the true spirit of Skinner and his behaviourist theory (1934/1976).

*What reward systems have you used and what were you rewarding?*

As teachers, you will recognize the positive and negative effects of running a reward system. Do you recognize the following and where do you position yourself on reward systems?

- They work well when the teacher's presence is felt.
- They appeal to those children who have a competitive nature.
- They encourage team spirit or do they?
- Not all children find themselves in a position to compete.
- Fellow housemates can apply a lot of unpleasant peer pressure in the name of competition.
- They can be very public declarations of success and failure (wall charts).
- Some teachers remove house points for unconnected misdemeanours.
- Should they be used for good work, behaviour, effort and tasks completed or only one of these?
- They are open to manipulation by the teacher, which may be seen as unfair.

Research by Dunmore (2009, cited in Bloom) on the effect of reward on secondary school pupils found that rewards improved behaviour but once rewards were withdrawn, poor behaviour returned. Also, withdrawing rewards for good work caused work, in some cases, to be even worse than when the rewards were introduced. Overall, she found that rewards reduce intrinsic motivation and they often provided little feedback so students could not improve their performance. On the positive side, she found that verbal praise was more successful, particularly when comments were given on improving competency and giving students the opportunity to comment on their completed tasks. A shift in autonomy towards the student with the teacher encouraging self-reflection appeared to be more motivating and productive.

Few teachers consider moving on from extrinsic reward. Independent learners are frequently mentioned but one has to question whether many teachers make a conscious effort to encourage pupil independence or leave them 'teacher dependent'?

There exist examples of schools in which no reward system exists, others where the only reward is the teacher's praise. Many teachers feel they need the reward system to support their control of behaviour and promotion of good work. This leaves the teacher in a dilemma. Do you introduce a reward system for initial control and then withdraw it with the possible effects observed by Dunmore or do you move gradually to giving more autonomy to students?

If we combine Maslow's hierarchy with knowledge of independent learners we could consider how one can adapt reward situations to encourage independence.

Ensure children:

- have a comfortable work space
- are well fed and healthy
- are successful
- grow in confidenceare respected
- are challenged.

They have opportunities to:

- be part of a working group
- be creative
- be reflective and evaluative of their own performance
- try different approaches
- organize their own work.

*If the reward system is up and running, how would you move children to self-reward and intrinsic motivation?*

Maybe we should recognize reward for what it is, an intermediate stage in developing independence.

# References and further reading

Black, P. and Wiliam, D. (1998) *Inside the Black Box: raising achievement through classroom assessment*, London: Kings College

Bloom, A. (2009) 'Beware the carrot: rewards don't work', *Times Education Supplement*, 13 November

Maslow, A. (1943) 'A theory of human motivation', *Psychological Review*, 50:4, 370–96

Skinner, B. (1976) *About Behaviourism*, New York: Vintage Books

[For more reading on independent learning, see Chapter 4.]

# Part II
## The Curriculum

13 Should we be teaching a second language to children under seven?    53

14 Is drama a luxury in the primary classroom?    57

15 Is there a place for picture fiction with children over seven?    61

16 Does correct spelling really matter?    65

17 Is it possible to make mathematics real and meaningful in the classroom?    69

18 How can questioning create thoughtful reflection and learning in mathematics?    73

19 Is physical education more than just being physically active?    78

20 Should ICT be taught as a subject, used as a learning tool or is there a need for both?    83

21 Should children be learning to make art or learning through art?    87

Each subject has many aspects that could be considered when teaching in the primary school. It would not be possible to discuss all the issues that arise from teaching content. This section contains a sample of topics where different opinions are held and seeks to question why we choose to approach them in the way we do.

# Should we be teaching a second language to children under seven?

## 13

### Vikki Schulze and Anthony Clarke

In England, in an ever increasing multicultural society, it is arguably no longer acceptable to assume that the majority of pupils will arrive in school with only an improving knowledge and understanding of the English language and England. Instead, an increasing majority already come with skills and knowledge of other languages and cultures (Roberts, 2005; Merrell et al., 2011). Furthermore, this trend is set to increase (DfE, 2010). Currently, pupils do have an entitlement to learn a modern European language from the age of seven and throughout Key Stage 2 (seven to eleven years) (DfES, 2002, 2005). However, this not only potentially fails to capture and capitalize on pupils' latent language experiences and skills, but also misses other potential advantages of an earlier start to second language learning in pupils' school careers. In 2008 92 per cent of primary schools were providing languages at Key Stage 2 (Wade et al., 2009). The majority also already provide some kind of informal language learning experiences in Key Stage 1 (5–7 years) and the Early Years Foundation Stage (three to five years). The suggestion that language learning should start earlier than age seven is therefore not without precedent or support.

*What is your view on the benefits and drawbacks of learning another language at an earlier age in school?*

There is no doubt that as a nation, despite our burgeoning multicultural society in England, we continue to lag behind other countries in terms of linguistic competence (European Commission, 2008; The Wray, 2008). The global dominance of English arguably reduces the incentive to engage with other languages.

*To what extent is this true of yourself or other people you know?*

There is a danger that a 'why bother' attitude may continue unless young children, and their teachers, are given meaningful purposes for engaging with other languages and cultures.

An important aspect of language learning is based on an appreciation of other cultures and understanding cultural diversity. The younger a child can appreciate and accept there are other nationalities and cultures, the better that understanding can grow and develop during the KS2 years. The teacher of 3–7-year-olds is in an ideal situation to start the pupils' intercultural journey. While the government's publication, *The Key Stage 2 Framework for Languages* (DfES, 2005), went some way to support intercultural understanding, nevertheless, children under seven have an enormous capacity to appreciate differences without bias and to develop their skills of empathy and tolerance (Jones and Coffey, 2006; Kirsch, 2008).

Most people would agree that there are benefits to speaking another language. Have you heard the question 'If only I had studied a language at school?' While it is never too late to learn a language, by the time such regrets may set in, it is often perceived to be too late to do anything about it. However, research into early language acquisition and optimum age theories remains largely inconclusive (Edelenbos et al., 2006).

*At what age did you start learning another language? What were the relative merits of this?*

There does appear to be a general consensus that young children do:

- demonstrate a passion, interest and aptitude for language learning
- have a physiological advantage in terms of pronunciation
- potentially have a longer period of time to develop their knowledge and use of other languages
- have the potential to apply an array of skills acquired during the language learning process to enhance their learning in other areas of the curriculum.

*Consider what kinds of transferable skill these can be for learning and for knowledge.*

Often, early experiences of language learning can include irrelevant vocabulary, meaningless phrases that are out of context, dull repetition and fear! Children under seven do not generally possess the fear and reluctance older learners can have. Wray (2008) suggests that young language learners have a tendency to just 'get on with it' in a holistic way, while older language learners display more of a tendency to unpick and repack the language. This can lead to more mistakes as languages are not always that logical.

*What kind of fears have you experienced in a language lesson? How much do you think such fears put teachers off?*

Younger children love to mimic, copy and play with sounds which they remember (Hood and Tobutt, 2009). They do this when learning their mother tongue and it is integral to the development of phonic awareness. Many language-learning activities are based on creative repetition and provide a broader range of sounds to experiment with. During a recent workshop on Chinese New Year to six-year-olds, trainee teachers noted how quickly the pupils learnt new words and sounds. Pupils had no previous experience of Mandarin yet by the end of the session they could repeat certain words with accuracy. Similarly some supervised trainee teacher research found that pupils of six and seven years appeared much more receptive towards languages than older pupils: 'The 6 and 7-year-olds were actually using the language in numeracy, manipulating it ... the 10-year-olds just repeated.'

The three to seven age range is, we would argue, a good time to make language learning holistic, meaningful and vibrant. Indeed, some of the best languages practice in Key Stage 2 'borrows' from good early years' practice. There are many relevant opportunities for pupils to use languages in real-life situations, where they are used 'just-in-time' as opposed to 'just-in-case' (Mehisto et al., 2008). Such examples include role play areas and classroom routines.

*Consider the benefits of using languages in this incidental way. How else can early years' teachers contribute towards an effective environment for language learning?*

Of course, all these things can be done in KS2. However, is it best left until then? The class teacher is also well placed to maximize the opportunities for early language learning, with their knowledge of the children, curriculum and appropriate pedagogy. First year trainee teachers were required to prepare story sacks in other languages and were amazed to discover the benefits of such a language resource for young learners. With minimal vocabulary and basic phrases based on popular stories, they delivered a range of successful lessons that did not require a great deal of linguistic competence.

There is no doubt that there are opportunities and advantages to be gained by involving younger pupils in second language learning. It is important, however, for teachers to recognize that the approach young learners bring to their language learning can be different to that of their own and for the need to match their teaching approach to the child's learning approach.

*How could you make language learning a motivating and successful experience for the young learner?*

# References and further reading

Cable, C., Driscoll, P. and Mitchell, R. (2010) *Language Learning at Key Stage 2 – a longitudinal study*, London: Department for Children Schools and Families (DCSF)

Department for Education (2010) *Schools, Pupils and their Characteristics* available at: http://www. education.gov.uk/rsgateway/DB/SFR/s000925/ index.shtml (accessed August 2011)

Department for Education and Skills (2005) *The Key Stage 2 Framework for Languages*, Nottingham: DfES Publications

DfES (2002) *Languages for All: languages for life. A strategy for England*, Nottingham: DfES Publications

Edelenbos, P., Johnstone, R. and Kubanek, A. (2006) 'The main pedagogical principles underlying the teaching of languages to very young learners', *Languages for the children of Europe. Published Research, Good Practice and Main Principles*, European Commission – Education and Culture, Culture and Communication: Brussels available at: http://ec.europa.eu/education/ languages/ languages-of-europe/doc137_en.htm and http://ec.europa.eu/ education/languages/pdf/doc631_ en.pdf (both accessed August 2011)

Hood, P. and Tobutt, K. (2009) *Modern Languages in the Primary School*, London: Sage

Jones, L. and Coffey, S. (2006) *Modern Foreign Languages: issues for teachers*, London: David Fulton

Kirsch, C. (2008) *Teaching Foreign Languages in the Primary School*, London: Continuum

Mehisto, P., Frigols, J. and Marsh, D. (2008) *Uncovering CLIL Content and Language Integrated Learning in Bilingual and Multilingual Education*, London: Macmillan Education

Merrell, C., Tymms, P. and Jones, P. (2011) *Changes in Children's Cognitive Development at the Start of School in England 2000–2006* available at: http://www.oxydiane.net/IMG/pdf/Baseline_ Assessment_2001_to_2006_v03.pdf (accessed August 2011)

Roberts, C. (2005) 'English as an additional language', *Times Educational Supplement*, 30 September

Sharpe, K. (2001) *Modern Foreign Languages in the Primary School: the what, why and how of early MFL teaching*, London: Kogan Page

Wade, P. and Marshall, H. with O'Donnell, S. (2009) *Primary Modern Foreign Languages: longitudinal survey of implementation of national entitlement to language learning at Key Stage 2 final report* (DCSF Research Report 127), London: DCSF.

Wray, A. (2008) 'The puzzle of language learning', *Language Teaching*, 41:2, 253–71

# Is drama a luxury in the primary classroom?

## Tracy Parvin

**14**

Several educationalists have suggested that the escalating importance with which the results of national testing are now being viewed by government, Ofsted and the media, has resulted in reduced teacher autonomy and primary school children being subjected to an increasingly prescriptive literacy curriculum (Pullman, 2003; Alexander, 2010; Ball et al., 2011). The drive towards the raising of standards in both reading and writing began in 1997 with the introduction of the National Literacy Strategy (NLS). It was designed as a literacy framework that 'specified the content, structure and teaching processes of a daily literacy hour' (Alexander, 2010, p. 209) and, although not statutory, was intended to complement and support the National Curriculum for English. The strategy at this time consisted of 1024 objectives, all of which were aimed at developing the teaching of reading and writing. None of these objectives made any reference to the development of children's speaking and listening skills. This omission, due possibly to speaking and listening not being a component of the testing procedures, signified the lower status afforded to oracy and highlighted a failure to understand its importance in children's literacy development.

*What profile does oracy have in your teaching?*

There is a wide range of research that explores how teaching approaches that build on children's linguistic progress enable metacognitive development. As Vygotsky stated: 'Thought is not merely expressed in words; it comes into existence through them' (1986, p. 218). This is an aspect of pedagogy that has been explored by Alexander (2008), who suggests that teachers who adopt a more dialogic practice encourage their classes to develop their thinking processes. Indeed, this is something that resonates with teachers, who are aware of this importance and, as a consequence, talk can be observed as a pedagogical feature in many primary classes.

*What speaking and listening activities do you consider to be important in developing children's thinking skills?*

In 2007 amendments were made to the literacy objectives of the Primary Framework, which gave greater emphasis to speaking and listening. An integral change to the speaking and listening strands was the inclusion of drama, which was afforded its own strand of learning objectives, thus demonstrating the belief that it is an essential component of literacy. Woolland (2010), however, suggests that, rather than be viewed in isolation, drama could be incorporated throughout the literacy curriculum, offering rich and powerful learning opportunities that would enhance the development of both reading and writing. This is an aspect of literacy pedagogy that has been extensively researched by academics such as Whitehead (2002), Cremin (2007), Woolland (2010) and Goouch and Lambirth (2011), to name but a few. All are unanimous in their belief that encouraging children to explore literature through drama imbues an understanding of narrative structures, characters, motives and themes, thus facilitating a collaborative construction of the meaning of the story and supporting the development of inference and deduction. Woolland (2010), however, emphasizes that drama conventions need to be carefully planned and devised so as to ensure that children become active and speculative readers immersed in the stories that they are interpreting and creating. Although a simple re-enactment that follows the original structure of the narrative might be an enjoyable activity, the children are merely passive players who are following a set of given instructions, an approach that could limit and restrict not only their dramatic explorations but also their reading comprehension. The challenge for teachers is to identify the dramatic potential within the stories that will prompt children to interrogate the text, thus extending their understanding and engagement.

*What drama conventions do you think could be developed so as to encourage children's explorations of a story that would take them beyond simply decoding the words on the page?*

Encouraging children to explore literature through drama might not only impact on their reading ability, but might also have a positive effect on their approach to writing. In recent years, the writing curriculum has become ever more prescriptive, with schools buying into schemes that offer a standardized, formulaic methodology to the teaching of writing (Grainger, Goouch and Lambirth 2005). The focus is predominantly on how ideas are expressed, rather than the all-important production of ideas; the process is neglected in favour of the product.

The skill of presenting ideas in a written form to be viewed by an external audience should not be underestimated. Grainger et al. (2005) and Woolland

(2010) suggest that, by creating a cohesive literacy curriculum with its foundations in drama and which moves seamlessly between speaking, listening, reading and writing, some of these writing difficulties might be minimized. One particular method might be to develop writing in role, an approach that Cremin (2007, p. 122) believes leads to children's development as writers. The oral rehearsing and refining of ideas in a collaborative situation allows children to create meaning in a visual sense, thus enabling and enriching their written work.

*How could you use drama as a starting point to writing?*

It could be suggested that in today's educational climate where the pressures of accountability have resulted in instances of 'teaching to the test' (Ofsted, 2008; Alexander, 2010) and a prescriptive formulaic approach to both reading and writing, drama could be viewed as a luxury. However, it is useful to be reminded of Vygotsky's (1986) notion of thoughts coming into being through the spoken word and then to consider whether incorporating drama into the literacy curriculum might enhance children's ability to articulate their reading responses and generate ideas for their writing. This is an aspect of education supported by the 1999 NACCCE report, *All Our Futures*, which also stresses the importance of collaborative work in developing socially adept young people who have well-honed communicative and problem-solving skills. Viewed in this context, perhaps it could be argued that drama is less of a luxury and more of a necessity.

# References and further reading

Alexander, R. (2008) *Essays on Pedagogy*, Abingdon: Routledge

—(2010) *Children, their World, their Education: final report and recommendations of the Cambridge Primary Review*, Abingdon: Routledge

—Website at http://www.robinalexander.org.uk/ (accessed August 2011)

Ball, S., Perryman, J., Maguire, M. and Braun, A. (2011) 'Life in the pressure cooker – school league tables and English and mathematics teachers' responses to accountability in a results-driven era', *British Journal of Education Studies*, 59:2, 179–95

Cremin, T. (2007) 'Drama', in Cremin, T. and Dombey, H. (eds) *The Handbook of Primary English in Initial Teacher Education*, Cambridge: UKLA, NATE and Canterbury Christ Church University

Cremin, T., McDonald, R., Goff, E. and Blakemore, L. (2009) *Jumpstart! Drama: games and activities for ages 5–11*, London: RoutledgeDfEE, (1998) *The National Literacy Strategy Framework for Teaching*, London: Standards and Effectiveness Unit

DfEE (1999) *All our Futures: creativity, culture and education: report of the National Advisory Committee on Creative and Cultural Education*, Sudbury: DfEE

DfES (2006) *Primary Framework for Literacy and Mathematics*, Nottingham: DfES

Goouch, K. and Lambirth, A. (2011) *Teaching Early Reading and Phonics: creative approaches to early literacy*, London: Sage

Grainger, T., Goouch, K. and Lambirth, A. (2005) *Creativity and Writing: developing voice and verve in the classroom*, London: Routledge

Ofsted (2008) *Mathematics: understanding the score*, London: Office for Standards in Education

Pullman, P. (2003) 'Teaching and testing', in Powling, C., Ashley, B., Pullman, P., Fine, A. and Gavin, J. (eds) *Meetings with the Minister*, Reading: National Centre for Language and Literacy

Vygotsky, L. (ed.) Alex Kozulin, 1986) *Thought and Language*, Cambridge: MIT Press

Whitehead, M. (2002) *Developing Language and Literacy with Young Children*, 3rd edn, London: Paul Chapman

Woolland, B. (2010) *Teaching Primary Drama*, Harlow: Pearson

[http://www.ite.org.uk/ite_topics/index.html is a very useful site that explores a wide range of aspects of the teaching of English.]

# Is there a place for picture fiction with children over seven? 15

Susan Barrett

Picture books are commonplace in Reception and Key Stage 1 (5–7-year-olds) classrooms. Bright colours, attractive illustrations and perhaps few words would make them seem ideal for the novice reader. A prevalent idea in the twentieth century was that this support could eventually be removed so that older children have often seen such books as being 'babyish' (Marriott, 1998). If this idea seems familiar, then consider these questions for a moment: are pictures more than a prompt to understanding? Are they more than illustrations? Might they, in fact, require a complex, cognitive activity, as readers wrestle with words, pictures, the relationship between the two and the gaps in between (Evans, 1998)? In the fully formed visual narrative, in which the function of the text is generally linear, while that of the pictures is often not, lies a tension and the opportunity for almost unlimited possibilities for interaction between word and image (Nikolajeva and Scott, 2006). Consider this integration of pictures with narrative.

*Reading picture books is easy, or is it?*

Although pictures, unlike words, match what they depict, they require children to have sufficient cultural knowledge to understand the ways in which they represent something (Nodelman, 1988), so they must learn conventions such as dots for eyes and crescent shapes or circles for mouths along with the cultural associations with different moods that they represent. They then need to be able to read 'the text created by the interaction of verbal and visual information' (Nikolajeva and Scott, 2006, p. 4). The visual representation often tells part of the story that the words do not (Browne, 1994). Consider *Come Away from the Water, Shirley* by John Burningham. What different stories do text and pictures tell? Or read Anthony Browne's *Zoo* or *Voices in the Park*, where the clear dissonance between pictures and text enables children to grapple with the difficult concept of irony.

This is the notion of 'counterpoint', 'word and image filling each other's gaps, or, compensating for each other's insufficiencies' (Nikolajeva and Scott,

2006, p. 139). If text or pictures, as in mere illustrations, fill all the gaps, then there is nothing left for the reader's imagination to do. If, however, they offer different information or even contradict each other, then multiple interpretations are possible (Martin and Leather, 1994). The child reader, here, then, is actively involved in the reading process, making meaning beyond merely decoding words on the page. When there are multiple narrative perspectives and unusual reading pathways as in David Wiesner's *The Three Little Pigs*, 'such books will produce readers that [sic] are alert and responsive' (Smith, 2008, p. 4).

*Would this be an important aim for your class and why?*

There are also the rhythms of picture book narratives to be considered. Nodelman (1988) noted the tensions created by the words which encourage accelerated reading and pictures which slow that down. He refers to the 'contrapuntal arrangement of mutual correction' (p. 243) when the two offer different insights into the same events and force the reader to revisit both in the light of the new interpretations gained from the different media. A text such as Roberto Innocenti's *Rose Blanche* has pictures that augment the limited understanding of the child narrator in World War II Germany. Here, a reader's ability to read two very different sign systems is required in order to understand the text, the context and particularly the ending fully.

*Can picture books support the reading process?*

First, consider their capacity to provide an equality of experience and access to a text in a way a written text alone does not (Bromley, 2003). The non-independent reader can respond to an image as much as a more experienced reader. For such readers in KS2 (7–11-year-olds) they can be challenged by the ethical questions raised by a book like Marsden and Tan's allegory, *The Rabbits*, in a way often denied to them in many 'catch-up' reading schemes. Pictures might also engage learners for whom English is not their first language, allowing them access to deeper meanings than many of the written texts offered to them often have (Coulthard, 2003). Exploration by children in upper KS2 of the wordless text *The Arrival* by Shaun Tan would also enable a deep empathy from pupils of the immigrant experience of some of their peers.

Reading a picture book is enjoyable, even 'an affective visual experience' (Doonan, 1993 p. 7), but how can it help develop reading skills? Research by Arizpe and Styles (2003) into how children aged four to eleven read visual texts found a sophisticated response: they 'read colours, borders, body language, framing devices, covers, endpapers, visual metaphors and visual jokes' (p. 224).

Looking at viewpoint in a picture, inferring meaning, considering style are all, in reading terms, higher order skills which involve 'deep thinking' (Arizpe and Styles, 2003) and therefore should be fostered in any classroom.

Intertextual links within picture books to other texts, film, television, painting and so on, prevalent in Browne's work for example, are an invitation by the authors to be actively involved in the reading process. In *Voices in the Park*, readers can speculate why Mary Poppins is in the sky or a Narnia-like lamppost is among the trees, but the primary narration is not dependent on these, so the reader with limited experience can enjoy it at one level, while others can read and reread it with added layers like an onion (Garner, 1977). Discussion and observations within the classroom can enable children to build on their own intertextual knowledge and provide them with valuable 'reading lessons' (Meek, 1988) about how authors construct narratives.

The picture book might appear 'to be the cosiest and most gentle of genres' (Egoff, 1981) and yet important subjects and themes can be explored: child homelessness in *Way Home* (Libby Hathorn), hatred and prejudice in David McKee's *Tusk Tusk*, state control of reading in John Light's *The Flower* or the ultimate taboo found in *Duck, Death and the Tulip* (Wolf Erlbruch). Their size and format enable them to be reread and discussed, moving children beyond a more literal level of comprehension. Children used to looking closely at picture fiction are far more likely to become sophisticated readers of other multi-layered texts in different contexts (Buckingham, 2003). As a professional, might you now be able to justify their position at the heart of the child's reading experience throughout primary school allowing them access to 'a pictured world full of ideas' (Doonan, 1993)?

# References and further reading

Arizpe, E. and Styles, M. (2003) *Children Reading Pictures: interpreting visual texts*, London: Routledge

Bromley, H. (2003) 'Putting yourself in the picture', in Arizpe, E. and Styles, M. (2003) *Children Reading Pictures: interpreting visual texts*, London: Routledge

Browne, A. (1994) 'Making picture books', in Styles, M., Bearne, E. and Watson, V. (eds) (1994) *The Prose and the Passion*, London: Cassell

Buckingham, D. (2003) *Media Education: literacy, learning and contemporary culture*, Cambridge: Polity Press

Coulthard, K. (2003) '"The words to say it": young bi-lingual learners responding to visual texts', in Arizpe, E. and Styles, M. (2003) *Children Reading Pictures: interpreting visual texts*, London: Routledge

Doonan, J. (1993) *Looking at Pictures in Picture Books*, Stroud: Thimble Press

Egoff, S. (1981) *Thursday's Child*, Chicago: Chicago University Press

Evans, J. (ed.) (1998) *What's in the Picture? Responding to illustrations in picture books*, London: Paul Chapman

Garner, A. (1977) 'A bit more practice', in Meek, M., Warlow, A. and Barton, G. (1977) *The Cool Web: the pattern of children's reading*, London: Bodley Head

Marriott, S. (1998) 'Picture books and the moral imperative', in Evans, J. (ed.) (1998) *What's in the Picture? Responding to illustrations in picture books*, London: Paul Chapman

Martin, T. and Leather, R. (1994) *Readers and Texts in the Primary Years*, Buckingham: Oxford University Press

Maybin, J. and Watson, N. J. (2009) *Children's Literature Approaches and Territories*, Milton Keynes: OUP

Nikolajeva, M. and Scott, C. (2006) *How Picture Books Work,* Abingdon: Routledge

Nodelman, P. (1988) *Words about Pictures: the narrative art of children's picture books*, Athens, GA: University of Georgia Press

Smith, V. (2008) 'Learning to be a reader: promoting textual health', in Goodwin, P. (ed.) (2008) *Understanding Children's Books: a guide for educational professionals*, London: Sage

## Children's texts

Browne, A. (1994) *Zoo*, London: Red Fox

—(1998) *Voices in the Park*, London: Doubleday

Burningham, J. (1992) *Come Away from the Water, Shirley*, London: Red Fox

Erlbruch, W. (2008) *Duck, Death and the Tulip*, Wellington: Gecko Press

Hathorne, L. (1994) *Way Home*, London: Andersen Press

Innocenti, R. (2004) *Rose Blanche*, London: Red Fox

Light, J. (2006) *The Flower*, Swindon: Child's Play

Mckee, D. (2006) *Tusk Tusk*, London: Andersen Press

Marsden, J. and Tan, S. (2008) *The Rabbits*, Sydney: Hachette Australia

Meek, M. (1988) *How Texts Teach What Readers Learn*, Stroud: Thimble Press

Tan, S. (2007) *The Arrival*, London: Hodder Children's Books

# Does correct spelling really matter?

## 16

### Caroline Tancock

> Hello, I am cleening out and unbloking gutters in the road oppersite yours this weekend. If you would like yours cleened please call … for a Free Qwote.

On first receiving this note through my letterbox, I initially found it rather irritating due to all the spelling errors. But then began to wonder whether it really actually mattered that these spellings were incorrect. After all, I had understood quite clearly the message the author was trying to get across. This led me to reflect on how important it actually is that children spell correctly and whether we emphasize the need for correct spelling too much.

Spelling does seem to generate much debate especially relating to the way it is taught in the classroom. The traditional way of learning to spell words was for it to be taught as a separate skill from writing and for children to learn and practise spellings from lists and weekly spelling tests and indeed this strategy still exists in many schools today. The problem is that a child may well be able to replicate the word for the purposes of the test but are then unable to spell the words correctly in any writing conducted in the future. This is mainly because the rote learning of the spelling results in its being taken out of any context. Also if spelling lists and tests worked then surely adults would not be spelling incorrectly – but clearly they are, as the gutter-cleaning note demonstrates. We need to be asking ourselves – what is important about helping children to spell words in their writing?

There can be no doubt that learning to spell in English is a complex matter. The English language has so many different historical influences – Latin, Greek, Celtic, Norman, French, Old Norse, American and European – that it can seem as if there are few consistent spelling rules or any coherent patterns in the construction of the words. Users of the English language are also willing to adapt words, adopt new words, spellings and language structures and this is even more apparent with the new forms of communication such as text messaging and tweeting in the current technological age. As with all languages, English is also constantly evolving and subject to influences from across the globe. However, it is this adaptability and global nature that makes English the successful and exciting language that it is.

Perhaps we need to start by considering what 'spelling' actually means. Kress (2000) defines spelling as knowing how to write words correctly. But this implies that being able to spell words is just a case of remembering the correct sequence of letters, hence the strategy of learning from spelling lists. But Kress continues by pointing out that many of the spelling rules relate to the sounds in the word and their corresponding written form:

> If spelling is simply a matter of reproducing, correctly, the remembered sequence of letters that make a written word, then all this stuff about the relation to the 'sound' of language is quite beside the point. (Kress, 2000, p. 1)

*What is the link between the sounds in the words (phonics) and that of spelling and is children's ability to learn how to spell related to how the spoken language is written down and ultimately to reading?*

The current focus on using phonemic strategies defines spelling as the segmentation of words into their constituent phonemes or sounds; that is, how the sound of the word corresponds to how it looks when written on the page. This definition sees the teaching of spelling as being clearly associated with the teaching of reading. Reading is concerned with the decoding of written language while spelling and writing are concerned with encoding written language. If children are to use their phonological awareness to learn to spell, and there is a clear link between reading and spelling, then they need to have the opportunity to play with language. Interest in words and word play will help to generate correct spelling. Bryant and Bradley's (1985) work on detecting rhyming words and their link to reading competence and Goswami's (1999) research on onset and rime highlight the important role of the rhythm of words and an awareness of syllables in children's spelling development.

*What is your experience of the links that children make between these aspects of reading and spelling?*

From the research just identified it appears that as children write, they engage in an active process of spelling words based on their knowledge of the visual representation of words and how the letters and sounds combine. If children are to develop their understanding and knowledge of spelling they need to be given the opportunity to try out the spelling even if they get it wrong and we need to encourage them to invent spellings for words they don't know. Children's spelling development takes time and it is through the act of writing that spelling will become more sophisticated, leading to correctness. Frank Smith (1982) argued that children should be given the opportunity to write and put their ideas into words even if this is before they can spell the words. Concerning inventive spelling, he stated that learning to spell takes time and begins with misspelling. He continues by suggesting that children who write only the words they know how to spell end up writing very little.

*Do you agree with Frank Smith's viewpoint?*

Wray and Medwell (2008) maintain that the teaching of spelling is more beneficial if it is done so in an enquiring way and Bearne (2002) suggests that spelling is best developed through experimentation with writing and experience. So while there may be a tendency to view spelling as being just about words this may not be the case, instead spelling can be considered to be inextricably linked to writing itself. This suggests it makes sense for children to learn about spelling through the actual act of writing. Indeed, Kress (2000) adds that the rules of spelling don't start from the sound and then guide to writing but instead it is the other way round – spelling rules start from writing and guide to the letter sequences in sound.

The key to helping children understanding spelling conventions is to see it as part of language study as a whole (Bearne, 2002). If children are to gain confidence and ability in their spelling then we as teachers need to recognize that spelling is an integral part of writing and not separate from or dominant in the writing process (Bearne, 2002). The Centre for Literacy in Primary Education study by O'Sullivan and Thomas (2007) found that children's spelling developed as they wrote more widely and if children's writing experiences were limited then their spelling development was adversely affected.

Children do need to realize that spelling is important but as with 'real writers' they also need to recognize that spelling doesn't dominate the writing and it can be addressed once the content and ideas are formulated. Any initial response to a piece of writing should always focus on the content and meaning and not the correctness of the spelling.

*As teachers do we put meaning first and develop spelling in meaningful contexts?*

Perhaps then we need to look at our attitudes towards spelling. While we need to consider carefully how we help our pupils make sense of the English words and the spelling system we also need to respond to any spelling errors in a way that is appropriate for the needs of the child, the child's stage of development, the context of the piece of writing and the audience and purpose.

Meaning, however, is an absolutely essential element of writing and ultimately we need to emphasize meaning before correct spelling. Kress (2000) distinguishes between accurate spelling and correct spelling and claims that nearly all children spell accurately in the sense that they represent accurately the sound of the word into its written form. But this is not necessarily the correct spelling in terms of English spelling conventions. As teachers we should be embracing this as these accurate sounding spellings give us an insight into the child's thinking and is the starting point for working with children on the 'correctness'.

# References and further reading

Bearne, E. (2002) *Making Progress in Writing*, London: Routledge

Bryant, P. and Bradley, L. (1985) *Children's Reading Problems*, Oxford: Blackwell

Goswami, U. (1999) 'Causal connections in beginning reading: the importance of rhyme', *Journal of Research in Reading*, 22:3

Kress, G. (2000) *Early Spelling: between convention and creativity*, London: Routledge

Martin, T. (2010) *Talk for Spelling*, London: United Kingdom Literacy Association (UKLA)

O'Sullivan, O. and Thomas, A. (2007) *Understanding Spelling*, Oxford: Routledge

Smith, F. (1982) *Writing and the Writer*, London: Heinemann

Wray, D. and Medwell, J. (2008) *Extending Knowledge in Practice: primary English*, Exeter: Learning Matters

# Is it possible to make mathematics real and meaningful in the classroom?

## 17

Jon Wild

Educational research into teaching mathematics often champions the role of contextualized learning. Researchers have long suggested that engaging children in mathematical activities that have meaning for them is crucial (Hughes, 1986; Atkinson, 1992; Nunes and Bryant, 1996). The Primary National Strategy promoted solving problems in a context (DFES, 2006). Yet what is evident in primary school mathematics lessons is that the contextualization is often in the form of word problems, with some picture clues to facilitate visualization. However, whether this word problem format can truly enable the mathematics to become real for the children is debateable.

*What is your experience of teaching mathematical problems?*

It could be argued, with some justification, that the prevalence of word-based problems in the primary classroom will continue while national testing dominates the educational landscape of the English primary school, as this is where assessment involving word problems reaches its zenith. If this is the case, is there a way to work towards making mathematical problems more accessible to children?

One of the key issues with word problems is related to pupil interpretation of context. Are the given contexts realistic from a child's point of view? While word problems are framed to provide a context that adults consider accessible and meaningful for the children, it is evident that they are not always realistic for the children. Blinko (2004) argues that this kind of context fails to be meaningful for the children because the children are required to find meaning in a situation that is already created for them rather than the children responding to a real need. The hypothesis is that when children find a need to do the mathematics, this is what makes context meaningful. Even if the children do manage to understand the context and can see the reason for doing the mathematics, another difficulty that is evident from national tests is that choice of context used does not really reflect children's experience. For instance, in the question that follows (Figure 17.1), which is based on the kinds of question that appear in national test papers for 11-year-olds, why would these children ever need six bags of potatoes?

I have 4 bags of potatoes. Each bag weighs 2.5 kilogrammes

Calculate the total weight of 4 bags of potatoes.

**Figure 17.1**

It would also be interesting to find out how many children have actually been camping (Figure 17.2)!

Some children go camping

It costs £2.30 per child to camp each night. How much will it cost each child to camp for 6 nights?

**Figure 17.2**

If this is the case then a key challenge for the class teacher is to be able to generate situations in which children can really relate to the context.

*With the children you have worked with, what would be examples of real situations that could be utilized for mathematical problem solving?*

Askew (2003) distinguishes between situations where the problem is solved by directly acting on it and those that require children to interpret the word problem and create a scenario in which they can do the mathematics. Analysing this, and drawing on the work of Treffers (1991), O'Sullivan et al. (2005) highlight the process that children undertake to envisage the mathematics required from the problem, use the mathematical processes need to find a solution and then translate this back into a solution that fits with the real context in which the problem was framed. This adds another layer of complexity for the children. This is without even considering the issues raised by Newman (1977) about being able to read and understand the language of the problem, as well as determine the mathematics required to calculate an answer, do the calculation and then interpret any solution to make sure that it makes sense in the context. Taken from this perspective, we begin to see the challenges for children that word problems in alien contexts have to offer.

*At what stage do you think the problem-solving process breaks down?*

The Dutch implementation of realistic mathematics education (RME), developed initially by Freudenthal (1968) has a focus away from the written word problem, creating pictorial opportunities for children to view mathematics in contexts, allowing the children to have fewer difficulties in engaging with the mathematics. Alongside this is the aim of providing problems that the children can find some resonance with, whether this is because it reflects the situations children encounter in reality or whether it is something fictional to which the children can relate. These problems aim to draw the child in and enable them to engage with the immediate mathematics and then extend this to more generalized situations (O'Sullivan et al., 2005). While this approach does not eliminate some of the difficulties related to creating a mathematical model from the reality presented, the discussion generated from considering these situations appears to be a step forward.

Despite the value of this approach, many of these situations do not mirror how children engage with mathematics outside of school and it could be argued that these contexts remain rather contrived. Merttens (1997) suggests that children learn at home in a natural manner as a direct consequence of what they experience every day. There is no planned curriculum and the learning is initiated by the child as a direct consequence of their interests. This raises the issue of the role of the context itself; whether it is purely a vehicle for the learning objective or whether it becomes the learning objective. This could also be allied to the practicalities of embedding elements of the 'Using and Applying' strand of the National Curriculum within learning contexts.

*How might you find meaningful contexts for children to enable problem solving? Would these exist solely in mathematics lessons? How can you ensure that process is sufficiently understood to be transferable?*

A key question for the teacher is whether it is possible to generate in the school environment a context that has a natural realism for the children, that has meaning for them, supports them in identifying where the mathematics is and what the mathematics is, so that they can then do the mathematics and interpret their conclusion in a meaningful way.

# References and further reading

Askew, M. (2003) 'Word problems: Cinderellas or wicked witches?', in Thompson, I. (ed.) *Enhancing Primary Mathematics Teaching*, Maidenhead: Open University Press

Atkinson, S. (1992) *Mathematics with Reason*, London: Hodder & Stoughton

Blinko, J. (2004) 'Mathematics in context', *Mathematics Teaching*, 188, 3–9

Department of Education and Employment (DfEE) (1999) *The National Curriculum. Handbook for primary teachers in England. Key stages 1 and 2*, London: Qualifications and Curriculum Authority (QCA)

Department for Education and Skills (DFES) (2006) *Primary Framework for Literacy and Mathematics*, Norwich: Crown Copyright

Freudenthal, H. (1968) 'Why teach mathematics as to be useful?', *Educational Studies in Mathematics*, 1:1, 3–8

Hughes, M. (1986) *Children and Number*, Oxford: Blackwell

Merttens, R. (1997) 'Family numeracy', Thompson, I. (ed.) *Issues in Teaching Numeracy in Primary Schools*, Buckingham: Open University Press

Newman, A. (1977) 'An analysis of sixth grade pupils errors on written mathematical tasks', in Clements, M. and Foyster, J. (eds) *Research in Mathematics Education in Australia*, 1, 239–58

Nunes, T. and Bryant, P. (1996) *Children Doing Mathematics*, Oxford: Blackwell

O'Sullivan, L., Harris, A., Sangster, M., Wild, J., Donaldson, G. and Bottle, G. (2005) *Reflective Reader: primary mathematics*, Exeter: Learning Matters

Treffers, A. (1991) 'Didactical background of a mathematics programme for primary education', in Streefland, L. *Realistic Mathematics Education in Primary Schools*, Utrecht: Utrecht University

# How can questioning create thoughtful reflection and learning in mathematics? 18

## Paula Stone

The way we as teachers engage with children in the classroom is deeply embedded in our culture (Alexander, 2001) however, it is important to bear in mind the learning and teaching interaction between teachers and pupils is very complex. One would assume that questioning generates higher level thinking and discussion and maximizes the potential of a learning opportunity in the classroom and it is the teachers' ability to ask questions and, more importantly, respond to them that engages pupils, and promotes learning. However, the findings of several studies reveal that although teachers ask lots of questions they are rarely used to encourage elaborated ideas (Smith et al., 2004). Furthermore, Dillon (1981) found that too many questions can evoke anxiety and can actually make pupils dependent on their teacher and become passive learners.

*How can teachers and student teachers get it right?*

There is a wide range of research dating back over 100 years that has examined the number and purposes of questions teachers ask (Stevens, 1912; Haynes, 1935; Gall, 1970, all cited in Wragg and Brown, 2001). More recently, Wragg and Brown (2001) have suggested that a teacher asks on average 300 questions a day and of these 57% are manager- type questions, 35% are used to gather information or recall data and 8% are higher order questions that encourage children to reason and reflect on their learning. If this were the distribution in your own lesson, what changes would you make and why? Why not count the number and type of questions in one mathematics lesson and reflect on the impact on children's learning.

Focusing on those questions that are related to learning – recall questions are generally closed questions that have just one correct answer and open questions that usually offer opportunity for possible alternative responses. There is general agreement based on a wide range of academic research (Bloom, 1956; Wragg and Brown, 2001; Alexander, 2004; Hodgen and Wiliam, 2006) that open questions are more likely to encourage higher order thinking and lead to greater understanding.

Can you think of reasons why? Here are few suggestions, open questions: enable children to enter the activity at their own starting point based on their own ability; engage in mathematical dialogue and observe other people being mathematical; extend their conceptual knowledge or apply knowledge in new contexts and encourage children pose as well as solve problems.

*Consider the difference between*:

*Think of some examples you have used with children.*

What are four threes?
Tell me two numbers with a product of 12.

*And between these two*:

$45 + \Box = 60$
Here's the answer, what could the question be?

Think of some examples you have used with children.

Of course each type of question has its use and purpose and we as teachers need to consider when it is appropriate to use open or closed questions. However, research by Smith et al. (2004) found that in numeracy lessons teachers spent the majority of their time asking questions that were of a low cognitive level designed to channel pupils' responses towards a required answer. They found that only 10% of the questions were open and only rarely were teachers' questions used to ask pupils for more complete or elaborated ideas.

*So what constitutes a good question in a mathematics lesson? Discuss with a peer which of these questions is more likely to require recall or promote higher order thinking and why? When would it be best to use each type of question?*

What is this shape called?

Give me a definition of a triangle.

Draw me a triangle. Now draw another different one and another. What is the same and different about each one?

Askew and Wiliam (1995) advocate the blend of higher order and lower order questions that match the needs of the learning outcome and the children in the class. This is supported by Wragg and Brown (2001) who suggest that teachers have to choose what kinds of learning they want to promote and then choose the appropriate questions. For example, if it is a lesson in which you are mainly focusing on facts, rules and procedure, for example learning the times tables, you may be more likely to ask closed questions that relate to knowledge. Or, if it is a lesson in which you are focusing mainly on understanding of mathematical concepts such as examining the properties of shape or responding to a statement like 'An even number that is divisible by 3 is also divisible by 6', you will be more likely to use open questions that relate to analysis, synthesis and evaluation.

If we, as teachers, want to encourage thought and thoughtful responses from the children we need to plan appropriate questions based on the learning outcome – it is not good enough merely to rely on our ability to ask questions as issues arise spontaneously in the lesson. Planning what type of question you will use is just one aspect of effective questioning techniques. Do you ever plan how you are going to distribute your questions; how you are going to pitch the questions so that they match the needs of the pupils; and how you are going to respond when the child gives an answer? These are all crucial elements to effective questioning.

Wragg and Brown (2001) claim that it is easy for teachers to deceive themselves about how many children, and who, have answered the questions in their lessons. They suggest that questions should be directed so that more pupils are involved more of the time. Can you discuss some strategies that you have observed and what made them more or less effective?

*Discuss some strategies that you have observed and what made them more or less effective.*

However, it is neither the act of asking questions itself nor the type of question teachers ask that limits pupil response in mathematics lessons, but the feedback given in reaction to pupil responses that has the greatest impact (Smith et al., 2004). According to Alexander (2003), the English primary education system is:

> dominated by closed questions inviting recall, limited 'wait' time for pupil thinking, brief answers which deliver information rather than access speculation and problem-solving, feedback which praises and supports but does not diagnose and inform, many questions from teachers but few from pupils, and little systematic building upon answers in order to construct coherent lines of reasoning and enquiry. (p. 6)

Teachers sometimes fail to see the implications of their responses to children's answers to their questions. Some of the most common teachers' responses I have observed in mathematics lessons are when children's answers are ignored and the teacher moves on or the teacher acknowledges but terminates the response with evaluative feedback (e.g. yes, no, well done). Both of these responses are usually demonstrated because the answer was correct; or the answer was incorrect or inappropriate; or indeed if there is a deficit in the teacher's subject knowledge.

Teachers need to go beyond the use of initiation–response–feedback type interaction in mathematics lessons by asking open-ended questions and follow-up questions, including asking pupils to justify or explain their answer through the use of further prompting and probing questions. Prompts contain hints that can help children if they are stuck or having difficulty explaining their reasoning. This can be done by rephrasing the question using more simple language or linking the learning to children's experience; asking a sequence of questions or by providing new information:

> Can you describe the problem in your own words?
> Can you talk me through what you have done so far?
> What did you do last time?
> Is there something that you already know that might help?
> Could you try it with simpler numbers … fewer numbers … using a number line?
> What could you try next?
> Is it a reasonable answer/result?

Probing questions are an effective strategy to encourage children to think more deeply about their responses and give more precise or detailed responses. Some examples include:

> How do you know …?
> Why do you think that …?
> Do you have a reason …?
> Can you give me an example …?
> Is this always so …?
> Is there another way/reason/idea …?
> What if …? What if … does not …?
> Where is there another example of this …?
> What do you think happens next?

It is at this point that one might want to consider the use of wait time (Askew and Wiliam, 1995) or talk partners so that the individual child feels less pressured or you want to engage all the children in their learning.

To promote a classroom culture in mathematics where children are offered more opportunities to think and talk about their mathematics, you will need to consider your questioning style. Plan your questions based on the learning outcomes; think about whether you can use open questions instead of closed questions; anticipate how children may respond; and, most importantly, think about how you will respond appropriately to what pupils say. In this way, you can promote higher level thinking that maximizes the potential of a learning opportunity.

# References and further reading

Alexander, R. (2001) *Culture and Pedagogy: international comparisons in primary education*, Oxford: Blackwell

—(2003) *Talk for Learning: the first year*, Northallerton: North Yorkshire County Council.

—(2004) *Towards Dialogic Teaching: rethinking classroom talk*, Cambridge: Dialogos.

Askew, M. and Wiliam, D. (1995) *Recent Research in Mathematics Education*, London: HMSO

Bloom, B., Engelhart, M., Furst, E., Hill, W. and Krathwohl, D. (1956) 'Taxonomy of educational objectives: the classification of educational goals', in *Handbook I: cognitive domain*, New York: Longman

Dillon, J. (1981) 'To question or not to question in discussion', *Journal of Teacher Education*, 32, 51–5

Hodgen, J. and Wiliam, D. (2006) *Mathematics Inside the Black Box: assessment for learning in the mathematics classroom*, London: NFER Nelson

Kyriacou, C. and Issitt, J. (2008) *What Characterises Effective Teacher-initiated Teacher-Pupil Dialogue to Promote Conceptual Understanding in Mathematics Lessons in England in Key Stages 2 and 3?*, London: EPPI Centre, Institute of Education

Mercer, N. and Littleton, K. (2007). *Dialogue and the Development of Children's Thinking: a sociocultural approach*, London: Routledge

Mercer, N. and Sams, C. (2006) 'Teaching children how to use language to solve maths problems', *Language and Education*, 20:6, 507–28, 6AA

Myhill, D., Jones, S. and Hopper, R. (2006) *Talking, Listening Learning: effective talk in the primary classroom*, Maidenhead: Open University Press

Smith, F., Hardman, F., Wall, K. and Mroz, M. (2004) 'Interactive whole class teaching in the national literacy and numeracy strategies', *British Educational Research Journal*, 30:3, 395–411

Wragg, E. (1993) 'Teaching teaching', *Classroom Teaching Skills*, London: Routledge

Wragg, E. and Brown, G. (2001) *Questioning in the Primary School*, London: Routledge

# 19 Is physical education more than just being physically active?

Kristy Howells

This chapter will question whether physical education (PE) lessons are more than just being physically active. It will examine the current expectations of PE lessons and what it means to be physically active. It will explore beyond just being active and consider the future of PE within a child's life and the role of competition in school PE.

PE lessons have been targeted in recent years by the Department of Health (DofH, 2005) as a prime outlet for increasing childhood physical activity and reducing levels of obesity as one in ten children in England is obese (Roberts, 2011). Mayall et al. (1996) identified PE lessons as health focused when children and teachers were asked. The World Health Organization (WHO, 2008) suggested that increasing the number of PE lessons is the most direct way to increase pupils' physical activity. Fairclough and Stratton (2006) argue that PE lessons could be considered as being pure opportunities to get children physically active but Howells et al. (2010b) question whether it can be really that simple; are PE lessons just about being physically active?

The DofH (2005) and the WHO (2010) suggested that children should be physically active at a moderate to intense level for 60 minutes a day. Levels of physical activity are difficult to judge visually and moderate to vigorous levels of physical activity can be accumulated throughout the day (Gilson et al., 2001; WHO, 2010). This is important as children's physical activity participation is rarely lengthy and often spontaneous (Kolle et al., 2009). However, it is important for school, class teachers, the children and teacher educators to know what the children's existing physical activity levels are prior to suggesting any solutions or strategies for primary schools (Howells et al., 2009). It is likely that children's physical activity and experience of PE in school can help determine their engagement in lifelong physical activity. It is therefore difficult for teachers and parents to know when children are reaching these levels and to provide individual opportunities for this to occur.

*To what extent do you feel that individual needs are met in PE lessons and how this might happen?*

PE should encompass individual physical development, health and well-being and has a crucial role in primary school education as it is much more than just simply providing exercising opportunities for every child. Within primary school, children are at a stage where habits, likes and dislikes are formed (Howells et al., 2010a), therefore PE is more than just being physically active. Yelling et al. (2000) agree and suggest that physical activity is 'only one consideration of PE lessons and the National Curriculum of PE' (p. 62). The aims of the National Curriculum for PE (DfEE, 1999) were designed to promote the pupils' spiritual, moral, social, cultural and academic development that links closely to the Every Child Matters agenda (DfES, 2003). Learning about the benefits of physical activity within PE lessons can help aid a 'positive attitude towards a healthy and active lifestyle' (Yelling et al., p. 62). Doherty and Brennan (2007) also suggested that PE lessons are not just about being physically active but about developing and educating the child physically in a holistic manner. However, this is an enormous amount for a teacher to be able to achieve within two hours of physical education a week.

*How can knowledge of a healthy lifestyle be promoted in conjunction with PE lessons?*

A fully physically educated child will appreciate the benefits of PE including physical development. It is therefore vitally important that children have a positive experience of PE during school, from primary school onwards, to increase confidence and self-esteem as well as physical capability. Pupils will then understand the benefits of regularly participating in exercise and will become comfortable about wanting to continue into later life. To assist in meeting this goal is the need for positive, motivated and enthusiastic role models (Howells, 2007).

Price (2008) believes these benefits of PE to the whole child should not be underestimated, suggesting PE plays a strong role in children's physical, social, affective and cognitive development. Alder (2000) identifies enjoyment as the key to children's learning, with Hirt and Ramos (2008) suggesting fun as potentially the central focus of PE lessons. Yet the National Association for Sport and Physical Education (2005) states that nowhere within the PE National Curriculum (DfEE, 1999) is 'fun' defined as an expected outcome. At their best, PE lessons can play an important role in shaping the character of a child, forming a supportive, honourable and considerate individual (Flemming and Bunting, 2007). Through communication that occurs within

PE lessons children are also able to create and consolidate friendships (Flemming and Bunting, 2007), to construct positive relationships and stronger communication skills. Raymond (1998) suggests that having 'silence' in PE lessons is a misconception and there is rarely a need for it though it is often used by teachers who are not as confident and wish to control the learning environment.

*To what extent is this more holistic approach to PE promoted in your school?*

It can be argued that international sporting events, particularly those being hosted in a country, increase the wish for competition and certainly the search for talent. This second phenomenon has been noted by Marsden and Weston (2007). However, it has to be questioned whether it is the role of primary schools to respond to this expressed need? Do teachers have the knowledge to promote gifted sportspeople and is there really room in the curriculum for coaching without alienating a huge proportion of the rest of the class (Manners and Carroll, 1995)? Whittingdale (2008) is unconvinced by the role of PE lessons in producing gifted athletes, stating that children who are particularly adept cannot and do not receive the required level of teaching and training in a setting where inclusion of the whole class is essential. In fact, competition is a double-edged sword in school. Whilst it brings glory to individuals and can be very motivating it can also have the opposite effect on the rest of the class. Humphrey (2002) warns of the need to pay attention to the negative effects that PE lessons can have on social skills through competition and through the constant emphasis on talent. Lord Coe (2011) summarized the vision of the Olympics as 'changing the lives of young people through sport', but we must be wary of how this vision is interpreted in school.

*How does a school structure its PE to meet the twin objectives of inclusive PE and supporting gifted children or does it not aim to do this?*

In conclusion, PE lessons have had a constant changing focus and value. It could be argued, as outlined, that PE lessons continue to have a very powerful influence on children and must remain prominent within the primary school curriculum. However, responses to political rhetoric and policy must be carefully considered so that children experience quality physical education and inclusion in the hope that physical activities will be part of the rest of their lives.

# References and further reading

Alder, H. (2000) *The Ultimate 'How to' Book: strategies for personal achievement*, Aldershot: Gower

Coe, S. (2011) 'It started with a bid', *Sport*, 217, 9–26

Department of Education and Employment (DfEE) (1999) *The National Curriculum. Handbook for primary teachers in England. Key stages 1 and 2*, London: Qualifications and Curriculum Authority (QCA)

Department for Education and Skills (DfES) (2003) *Every Child Matters: change for children* available at: http://www.everychildmatters.gov.uk/publications/ (accessed September 2007)

Department of Health (DofH) (2005) *Choosing Activity: a physical activity action plan* available at: http://www.dh.gov.uk/prod_consum_dh/groups/dh_digitalassets/@dh/@en/documents/digitalasset/dh_4105710.pdf (accessed October 2009)

Doherty, J. and Brennan, P. (2007) *Physical Education and Development 3–11: a guide for teachers*, Abingdon: Routledge

Gilson, N., Cooke, C. and Mahoney C. (2001) 'A comparison of adolescent moderate-to-vigorous physical activity participation in relation to a sustained or accumulated criterion', *Health Education Research*, 16, 335–41

Fairclough, S. and Stratton, G. (2006) 'Effects of physical education intervention to improve student activity levels', *Physical Education and Sport Pedagogy*, 11:1, 29–44

Flemming, T. and Bunting, L. (2007) *PE Connections: helping kids succeed through physical activity*, Leeds: Human Kinetics

Hirt, M. and Ramos, I. (2008) *Maximum Middle School Physical Education*, Leeds: Human Kinetics

Howells, K. (2007) 'A critical reflection of the opportunities and challenges of integrating the Every Child Matters (ECM) agenda into teaching physical education (PE)', *Physical Education Matters*, 2:1, ii–iii

—(2011) 'A professional introduction to physical education' in Driscoll, P., Lambirth, A. and Roden, J. (eds) *The Primary Curriculum: a creative approach*, London: Sage

Howells, K., Wellard, I. and Woolf-May, K. (2009) 'Do physical education lessons increase physical activity levels of primary aged children? – preliminary findings', in MacPhail, A. and Young, A. (eds) (2009) 'Promoting physical education across schools and communities', in the *Proceedings of the Fourth Physical Activity Physical, Activity and Youth Sport Forum*, University of Limerick

Howells, K., Caple, A. and Jones, M. (2010a) 'Are boys more physically active than girls during a primary school day?', *Primary Physical Education Matters*, Autumn 5:3, xvii–xix

Howells K., Wellard I. and Woolf-May K. (2010b) 'Do physical education lessons contribute to children's physical activity levels?', in Enright, E. and Tindall, D. (eds) (2010) 'A shared vision for physical education, physical activity and youth sport', in the *Proceedings of the Fifth Physical Education, Physical Activity and Youth Sport (PE PAYS) Forum*, University of Limerick

Humphrey, J. (2002) *An Anthology of Stress: selected works of James H. Humphrey*, New York: Nova Publishers

Kolle, E., Steene-Johannessen, J., Klasson-Heggebø, L., Andersen, L. B. and Andersen, S. A. (2009) 'A 5-yr change in Norwegian 9-yr olds' objectively assessed physical activity level', *Medicine and Science in Sports and Exercise*, 41:7, 1368–73

Manners, H. and Carroll, M. (1995) *A Framework for Physical Education in the Early Years*, London: Falmer

Marsden, E. and Weston, C. (2007) 'Locating quality physical education in early years pedagogy', *Sport Education and Society*, 12:4, 383–98

Mayall, B., Bendelow, G., Barker, S., Storey, P. and Veltman, M. (1996) *Children's Health in Primary Schools*, London: Falmer

National Association for Sport and PE (2005) *Physical Education for Lifelong Fitness: the physical best teacher's guide*, 2nd edn, Leeds: Human Kinetics

Price, L. (2008) 'Creativity and gymnastics', in Lavin, J. (ed.) *Creative Approaches to Teaching Physical Education: Helping Children Achieve*, London: Routledge

Raymond, C. (1998) *Coordinating Physical Education across the Primary School: the subject leader's handbook*, London: Routledge Falmer

Roberts, M. (2011) 'Call to measure duration of obesity' available at: http://www.bbc.co.uk/news/health-14614209 (accessed August 2011)

Whittingdale, J. (2008) *London 2012 Games: the next lap – sixth report of session 2007–2008*, Vol. 2, London: The Stationery Office

World Health Organization (WHO) (2008) *School Policy Framework. Implementation of the WHO global strategy on diet, physical activity and health* available at: http://www.who.int/dietphysicalactivity/SPF-en-2008.pdf (accessed October 2010)

World Health Organization (WHO) (2010) *Global Recommendations on Physical Activity for Health* available at: http://whqlibdoc.who.int/publications/2010/ 9789241599979_eng.pdf (accessed October 2010)

Yelling, M., Penney, D. and Swaine, I. (2000) 'Physical activity in physical education: a case study investigation', *European Journal of Physical Education*, 5, 45–66

# Should ICT be taught as a subject, used as a learning tool or is there a need for both?

## 20

Nyree Scott

Each individual may have her own opinion with regard to the teaching of information communication technology (ICT) and the role ICT should play. Green (2011) sees it as, 'a subject in its own right with a history and a future' (p. 139). Increasingly within schools, however, ICT is being used by teachers not just for teaching, but also as a medium through which children can learn. This was evident when, during the 2010–11 school year, I observed eight different 'ICT lessons' being delivered by students who were following an ICT subject option on a primary teacher training route. Of those eight lessons, six chose to deliver their lesson using ICT to aid the children's learning; for example, a mathematics lesson that used MS Excel to collate and interpret data. Only two students chose to teach specific ICT skills; for example, how to create a database and used birds' features as an example of content. Although learning took place in all eight lessons, I was left asking which were the best learning experiences: the ones in which there was a need to use the software or teaching how the software works?

Learning in ICT isn't as straightforward an issue as it would at first appear. The less obvious but key issue isn't how ICT is taught, but how it is assessed to help the children develop further and enable them to be challenged in relation to their own abilities in the subject that can be at vastly different levels in a class of children. This 'digital divide' as described by BECTA (2001) can have far reaching consequences within the classroom.

*How do we keep track of a subject where children can enter school already in advance of or behind their peers?*

So, as we establish the place of ICT within the school curriculum we need to answer the question of what is meant by ICT. The National Curriculum is clear in its guidance for the teaching of ICT but this was written in 1988 and revised in 2000 and 2002 and is currently being updated. We move in a society with rapidly developing technology where most 'children grow up in technologically rich environments' (Price, 2009, p. 136) therefore the National

Curriculum will rapidly become dated in its content and expectations. What specifically do we need to teach pupils to develop their ICT knowledge while ensuring that we don't work at a level lower than they are capable of or exclude those who still do not have opportunities at home to access such things as the internet? And are schools absorbing the latest technologies into their classroom practice?

We need to consider not only how children best learn, but also the starting point at which children enter the classroom. Not all children will be entering school with the same level of ICT experience due to their socioeconomic status (BECTA, 2005). We also need to take into consideration e-safety, an area that was not considered when the National Curriculum was first written. Is there a place to embed what could be viewed as such an important area within another subject such as PSHE or should it be given the status it requires ensuring children are properly prepared for using 'electronic' technology? A point should perhaps be noted that in 2009 prior to the arrival of the coalition government, e-safety lessons were set to become compulsory in all primary schools by 2011.

The statistics are clear: the percentage of children of primary age who have access to or owned a computer has risen considerably over the past decade; from 1999 to 2009 the percentage of households owning a computer rose from 38 per cent to 75 per cent (Office of National Statistics (ONS), 2010). ChildWise (2008), however, puts this figure higher at 90 per cent of children aged five to sixteen having a computer at home and use of the internet. The amount of time children spend on the computer, playing games consoles or 'playing' on mobile phones or, in fact, owning a mobile phone has risen significantly in recent years.

*What are schools doing to address the needs of these digital natives as Prensky (2001) calls them?*

The introduction of the New Opportunity Fund (1999) and the resulting ICT boom brought about an influx of ICT suites being built into schools with enough computers for most classes to work one between two children. Timetables were drawn up and classes eagerly got to go to the ICT suite at least once a week for their ICT lessons. Perhaps the question that needs to be asked is this: what are the children doing once they get there?

*Consider the following two scenarios.*

Scenario 1: The children are being taken to the suite and shown how to use MS PowerPoint. During these sessions they could be shown how to open the software, save it and how to use various features within it. The children could then be left to 'play' with the software to develop an understanding of how it works and its limitations.

Scenario 2: The children are being taken to the suite to produce a talking book to be used by foundation children in their reading corner. The children have already discussed and made notes of the story they wish to write and once in the ICT suite are introduced to MS PowerPoint as the way on this occasion they are going to produce their book. They are shown the basic skills such as how to add text and pictures as well as how to link between pages by a button and how to embed sound. They are also told there are other features of the software that they may find beneficial but the tools shown are a good starting point. The pupils then set about writing their stories while adding features that they have been shown. A child may decide he wants to use a specific feature pertinent to his story and so asks if it is possible, peers or the class teacher can make suggestions.

Research has shown how children need to be given the opportunity to familiarize themselves with technology and teach themselves how it works (Price, 2009). Guidance by an adult may ensure that children do not become frustrated if unable to grasp what the technology is asking of them (Plowman et al., 2006). Children's acquired knowledge of the software could then be used in future tasks. In the second scenario, the children not only familiarize themselves with the software but also to have a need to use it. This brings us back to the original viewpoints on the role of ICT in primary schools. A further question to consider is the one Prensky (2001) asked, should we be teaching our children 'just in time' as they prefer to learn or 'just in case' as we prefer to teach them?

*What is your experience of the use of the ICT suite and how effective was the children's learning of ICT? What new ICT skills did they acquire and did they apply new skills to subject contexts and learn as a result of that application?*

ICT isn't just about computers, it's about many more technologies. Consider these suggestions on how ICT can be used to enhance the learning experience while developing the children's own ICT skills at the same time:

- Using a digital camera is not just about a snapshot of a classroom celebration. Think animation, enabling the ICT skills to be driven forward whilst enhancing learning in other areas. Consider how working within groups creates a 'dialogic space' (Wegerif, 2007) in which pupils can socially construct new insights and understanding. An animation of the lifecycle of a frog is more than just demonstrating secure knowledge of the process.

- Mobile recording devices enable pupils to share their ideas not only with a global audience through the use of podcasting but also with peers throughout the school and families who otherwise may not have the opportunity to see what their children are learning. Hot seating and interviews with historical figures or a radio show about the last school trip opens up a whole new world of learning while developing ICT skills along the way.
- Remote-controlled toys used from the Foundation Stage are a basic introduction to the world of programming. Programming your 'toy' to move from one area on the carpet to another area sets the stage for future programs such as Logo, Lego Mindstorms or Scratch.

These, of course, are just a small example of how ICT can be used within the primary classroom. The computer is an integral part of ICT, but sometimes we need to step away to ensure we are providing the pupils with the opportunity to develop as learners using ICT not just as a tool but also in teaching other subjects.

# References and further reading

BECTA (2001) *The Digital Divide: a discussion paper* available at: http://www.cse.dmu.ac.uk/~ieb/ digital%20divide.pdf (accessed April 2012)

—(2005) *Already at a Disadvantage? ICT in the home and children's preparation for primary school* available at: http://www.ioe.stir.ac.uk/ research/ projects/interplay/docs/already_at_a_ disadvantage.pdf (accessed October 2011)

ChildWise (2008) *ChildWise Monitor: the trends report*, Norwich: SMRC ChildWise.

Green, M. (2011) 'An introduction to information communication technology', Driscoll, P., Lambirth, A. and Roden, J. (eds) *The Primary Curriculum, a Creative Approach*, London: Sage

Office of National Statistics (ONS) (2010) available at: http://www.statistics.gov.uk/ downloads/ theme_social/familyspending2010.pdf (accessed October 2011)

Plowman, L., Stephen, C., Downey, S. and Sime, D. (2006) 'Supporting learning with ICT in pre-school settings', *Teaching and Learning Research Briefing* 15 available at: http://www.tlrp.org/ pub/documents/no15_ plowman.pdf (accessed October 2011)

Prensky, M. (2001) 'Digital natives, digital immigrants', *On the Horizon*, 9:5, 1–6

Price, H. (2009) *The Really Useful Book of ICT in the Early Years*, New York: Routledge

Wegerif, R. (2007) *Dialogic, Education and Technology: expanding the space of learning*, New York: Springer

# Should children be learning to make art or learning through art?

## 21

### Peter Gregory

This chapter discusses the question of whether primary school art lessons should focus on 'product' or 'process'. Looking into the classrooms of many primary schools, observers will be struck by the frequent displays of artworks by (often dead) 'famous artists', which may be surrounded by very similar-looking images produced by the pupils. Is this a good basis for studying art? The question really needs to be deconstructed to do justice to the answer. Should primary pupils learn about the works of artists? If so, who, and by implication, why? How does the emphasis on the finished artworks of others affect the processes by which children learn in art as a subject? How will all this affect the pedagogy of the teacher? These are questions for consideration, but first a different question.

*What is your observation of art in primary classrooms?*

The statutory curriculum for art in primary schools has since 1992 included a requirement to teach children about the artworks of other artists. At the time of writing, the most recent curriculum guidance document states: 'Pupils should be taught about differences and similarities in the work of artists, crafts people and designers in different times and cultures' (QCA, 1999, p. 16).

This seems to answer the first question in full: teachers teach about other artists because they are required to do so. The harder issues to consider are who is to be studied and why? There are no lists of artists provided in the statutory curriculum although an earlier version (DES, 1992) did contain such information in the examples published within it. This 'canon' of artists (Gretton, 2003) was heavily criticised by some as limiting and resulted in only a reinforcement of an 'orthodoxy', eroded aspects of creativity, discounted certain forms of art and artists – tending to restrict the focus to the works of 'dead, white, European male artists' (Steers, 2004). The subsequent versions of the curriculum documents moved away from reinforcing this 'canon' but the influences are still evident in schools and this legacy is questioned by some (Dixon, 2010, cited in Alexander, 2010).

*Do you consider a particular group of artist should be studied and can you say why?*

Having established that teachers must teach about artists, we ought to pause to consider who should define who these might be. There is considerable evidence that primary teachers tend to focus on the artists that they know about and as a result exclude reference to contemporary artists or works from other cultures (Burgess, 2003; Downing and Watson, 2004; Page et al., 2006; Ofsted, 2009). This may limit the outworked vision of the professional teacher who sets their sights on affecting the future and allowing children to explore their world. Without considering the effect that a narrowed 'canon' of artists might have on this exploration, teachers could weaken understanding of twenty-first century art.

*What range of art does your choice of artists offer both in time, style and message?*

Prior to the first National Curriculum documents for England, art had been taught in schools as primarily a process-driven subject (Clement and Tarr, 1992). Teachers would allow children to explore a wide variety of media and materials while they concentrated on teaching skills and techniques. This sounds as though I might be suggesting that this period was some kind of 'golden age' but actually the evidence does not substantiate such a view. Often class teachers had too little art teaching and experiences themselves in their training and, feeling underconfident themselves, minimized the activities in their classrooms. Some openly disliked the subject so avoided it altogether (Tickle, 1987).

Macdonald (2004) charts the impact of changing societal context and educational philosophies and beliefs in moulding the ways in which art has been understood and taught as a result. In the late nineteenth century art in schools was usually taught as a 'drawing class' and the pedagogy employed concentrated on transmitting the technical knowledge and/or skill from the teacher to the pupil in a particular way. Perhaps this is the way that you experienced art in your own school career? The issue of the philosophy of art education often remains affected by the teacher's learned pedagogy. Teachers tend to teach what they believe in.

*What are your beliefs about how art should be taught? Is your art teaching based on technical skill building, modelling of great artists, a mixture of the two or a third approach?*

I would like to briefly describe and contrast two distinct approaches to art education. I have seen both in contemporary classrooms, justified by the same curriculum but reflecting quite different belief systems by either the individual teacher concerned or the collective staff team of the school involved.

The first could be described as 'transmissional' and broadly link to the work of Skinner (1950) and others on the importance of behaviourism as a mechanism for learning. The teachers follow published schemes of work and reinforced the notion that the pieces of art work produced represent the 'product' that is what should be measured and assessed (Ofsted, 2009). This product approach is often seen where inexperienced educators follow the script for successful art lessons and use the published images of example end products as the guide for children to follow, aiming to achieve similar results or even simply copy them. In so doing, the teacher provides a point against which the success of the art activity can be measured. There is therefore a 'right answer' or desirable product and many possible 'wrong answers' (Littledyke and Huxford, 1998). The pupils receive the transmitted message from the teacher and work towards this end.

The second scenario has elements of 'constructivism' associated with it as children will often be asked to consider their ideas and ask questions as they look more closely at artists' work. Hoye (1998) considers the principle of the child as an artist in their own right. This is not a new concept and has been explored by Dewey (1934) and others across the twentieth century. If a pupil can gain aesthetically by looking at the work of adult artists, then the activity is no longer about the resulting product made by the child, but rather the enriching nature of the opportunities provided. Matthews (2003) argues strongly that the main influence in the art work produced by children is, first, who they are as individuals and, second, the opportunities for reflective development allowed them by the adults who supported or teach them. There is therefore no 'right' or 'wrong' answer. In short, the opportunities for looking at and considering the work of adult artists, it could be argued, are best understood as enriching and provocative activities. In some classrooms, this form of exploration is revealed but the display of children's work may bear little resemblance to that of the artists studied.

*What kind of teacher of art do you think you will be? Should artistic endeavour be measured and, if yes, what criteria would you use?*

Perhaps this question has not arisen before? It is important to consider and reflect on it as you observe art being taught as well as experiment in your own teaching.

# References and further reading

Addison, N., Burgess, L., Steers, J. and Trowell, J. (2010) *Understanding Art Education*, Abingdon: Routledge

Alexander, R. (ed.) (2010) *Children, Their World, Their Education: final report and recommendations of the Cambridge Primary Review*, Abingdon: Routledge

Burgess, L. (2003) 'Monsters in the playground: including contemporary art', in Addison, N. and Burgess, L., *Issues in Art and Design Teaching*, London: Routledge Falmer

Clement, R. and Tarr, E. (1992) *A Year in the Art of a Primary School*, Corsham: NSEAD

Cox, S. and Watts, R. (eds) (2007) *Teaching Art and Design 3–11*, London: Continuum

DES (1992) *Art in the National Curriculum (England)*, London: DES

Dewey, J. (1934) *Art as Experience*, New York: Minton Balch

Dobbs, S. (2003) *Learning in and Through Art*, Los Angeles: Getty Publications

Downing, D. and Watson, R. (2004) *School Art: what's in it?*, Slough, NFER

Gregory, P. (2011) 'Subject leaders of art and design in primary schools', *AD: The National Society for Education in Art and Design*, Spring, 1, 19

Gretton, T. (2003) 'Loaded canons', in Addison, N. and Burgess, L., *Issues in Art and Design Teaching*, London: Routledge Falmer

Herne, S., Cox, S. and Watts, R. (eds) (2009) *Readings in Primary Art Education*, Bristol: Intellect

Hoye, L. (1998) 'Let's look at it another way: a constructivist view of art education', in Littledyke, M. and Huxford, L., *Teaching the Primary Curriculum for Constructive Learning*, ondon: David Fulton

International Society for Education through Art (InSEA) available at: www.insea.org (accessed September 2011)

Littledyke, M. and Huxford, L. (1998) *Teaching the Primary Curriculum for Constructive Learning*, London: David Fulton

MacDonald, S. (2004) *The History and Philosophy of Art Education*, Cambridge: Lutterworth Press

Matthews, J. (2003) *Drawing and Painting: children and visual representation*, London, Sage

National Society for Education in Art and Design (NSEAD) available at: www.nsead.org (accessed September 2011)

Ofsted (2009) *Drawing Together: art, craft and design in schools 2005–8*, London: Ofsted

Page, T., Herne, S., Dash, P., Charman, H., Atkinson, D. and Adams, J. (2006) 'Teaching now with the living: a dialogue with teachers investigating contemporary art practices', *International Journal of Art & Design Education*, 25:2, 146–55

QCA (1999) *Art and Design: the National Curriculum for England*, London: QCA

Skinner, B. F. (1950) 'Are theories of learning necessary?', *Psychological Review, 57*, 193–216

Steers, J. (2004) 'Art and design', in White, J., *Rethinking the School Curriculum: values, aims and purposes*, London: Routledge Falmer

Tickle, L. (ed.) (1987) *The Arts in Education: some research studies*, Beckenham: Croom Helm

# Part III
## The Wider World

22 Why do children and teachers need to develop a multicultural and global perspective?   93

23 What makes stereotypes pernicious?   97

24 Should we teach children about current affairs?   100

25 Maps are increasingly being used by children but do these maps tell the truth?   103

Improved communication and the expanse of the media have brought the rest of the world into everyone's home and school. We have travelled far from the textbook stereotypes that children studied in the 1950s. At the same time an increased awareness of our planet and its people raises questions about what we should be teaching in the primary school. This part considers some of the issues arising from developing a global curriculum.

# Why do children and teachers need to develop a multicultural and global perspective?

**22**

Tony Mahon

It is clear that we now live in an increasingly interdependent, global community in which events in one part of the world can have a dramatic impact on daily lives closer to home; and, conversely, our choices and actions can affect the lives of people on the other side of the world. For example, the decisions we make about the energy we use can contribute to changing rainfall patterns or sea levels in countries thousands of miles away, which can have an impact on the crops that are grown and exported for sale in supermarkets in England and other countries.

We can also see that many local communities are much more diverse than a mere 10 or 20 years ago. Within primary schools in England some 25% of children originate from minority ethnic backgrounds and some 16.8% of children have a first language that is not English (School Census, DfE, 2011). This is a figure that has almost doubled in the last 15 years. It is also predicted that in the near future one in four jobs will involve international trade or working (DFID, nd).

One of the most significant challenges that teachers now face is how to prepare young children to develop knowledge, skills, values and attitudes that will enable them to succeed and make valuable contributions to the society of the future within rapidly, ever-changing local and global worlds. It can be argued that this involves children and teachers developing a multicultural and global perspective so that both are better informed and better prepared to face the challenges of living and working in a multicultural, global environment.

*Do you agree that there is a need to develop 'both' multicultural and global perspectives?*

There is a subtle difference between 'multicultural' and 'global' that needs to be recognized because many of our children live in and interact directly or indirectly with a multicultural community as well as being part of the wider global community. Children need to develop an understanding of what this means for them. A global perspective focuses mainly on 'what connects us to the rest of the world. It enables learners to engage with complex global issues and explore the links between their lives and people, places and issue throughout the world' (QCA, 2007, p. 2). However, a multicultural perspective is more closely related to understanding ourselves by considering how our values and actions affect our relationship to the multicultural community within which we live and how they affect our view of both the local and wider world. Teaching with a multicultural and global perspective will encourage the development of a positive understanding and appreciation of the value and uniqueness of other cultures as well as one's own. This is crucial to counteract the danger of children forming negative stereotypes of those from other ethnic groups and cultures.

*How can teachers adopt a multicultural and global approach when they teach in a school with very low ethnic diversity?*

This can be perceived as a challenge; however, there are now many ways in which schools can begin to adopt a more global, multicultural outlook on teaching and learning. One of the most effective ways of doing this is for schools to establish partnerships with schools in other countries. The Department for Education and Skills (DfES, 2004) suggests that establishing international links can be a powerful way to support the global dimension across the curriculum by bringing issues to life for children in both countries. Schools can find considerable support to establish such partnerships from a number of sources. An excellent starting point is the British Council's International School Award scheme. This provides guidance, support and resources to help schools develop policy, establish partnerships with schools in other countries to collaborate on international learning projects and activities, and engage in curriculum-based work across a range of subjects. Schools that participate can also gain accreditation for the international school award.

*What else can teachers do to ensure that a multicultural and global perspective is fully embedded in the curriculum and impacts on the learning of all children?*

To develop an effective multicultural and global perspective that is embedded not only in the curriculum but also informs the ethos of the whole school, it is important that international or multicultural activities are not seen to be tokenistic one-off events. Banks (2007) outlined four levels of integration of multicultural content in the curriculum:

- Contributions approach. Contributions are one-off events that might involve highlighting heroes, festivals and other discrete cultural elements, e.g. reading a story from another culture, placing posters around the school showing children from different cultures or with words of welcome in different languages or learning about festivals from other cultures such as Chinese New Year or Diwali.

- Additive approach. This involves adding content, concepts, themes and perspectives to an existing curriculum without changing its structure, e.g. studying a range of stories from a particular culture within the existing curriculum.
- Transformative approach. This does involve restructuring the curriculum so that children can view concepts, events and themes from perspectives of diverse ethnic and cultural groups, e.g. rather than studying an isolated myth, a new comparative unit may be developed that explores a variety of creation myths from a range of cultures.
- Action approach. This is a more dynamic socially conscious approach that involves children exploring social issues or problems in depth, making decisions and taking actions to help solve them, e.g. work collaboratively on projects that may range from letters of protest to a local newspaper about issues of bias or racism in the community.

*How might a school move from a contributions approach to a transformative or action approach?*

I would argue that a principled and systematic approach needs to be adopted. For example, the booklet *Developing the Global Dimension in the School Curriculum* (DfES, 2005) adopts such an approach by providing a conceptual framework and guidance for integrating the global dimension into the school curriculum at all phases from Foundation through Key Stages 1 and 2 (three to eleven years) and beyond. Eight key concepts are outlined, which can be used to support planning, teaching and evaluation.

These are global citizenship, conflict resolution, diversity, human rights, interdependence, social justice, sustainable development and values and perceptions. Higgins (2009, p. 52) argues that:

> Children are our future leaders and decision-makers, and making them aware of these concepts is paramount if we are to address global issues such as poverty, health, education and discrimination, and prepare children for life in the 21st century.

If we agree with her assertion then surely it is our responsibility as educators to take action to ensure that children are provided with the opportunities and support to develop such a multicultural and global perspective.

# References and further reading

Banks, J. and McGee Banks, C. (eds) (2007) *Multicultural Education: issues and perspectives*, 6th edn, New York: John Wiley

British Council (nd) *International School Award* available at: http://schoolsonline.britishcouncil.org/International-School-Award/about-ISA (accessed November, 2011)

Department for Education (2011) *School Census*, London: Crown Printers

Department for Education and Skills (DfES) (2004) *The DfES International Strategy: 'Putting the World into World-Class Education'*, London: Crown Printers

—(2005) *Developing the Global Dimension in the School Curriculum*, London: Crown Printers; available at: www.globaldimension.org.uk

Department for International Development (nd) *The World Classroom: developing global partnerships in education* available at: www.dfid.gov.uk (accessed November 2011)

Derbyshire Advisory and Inspection Service (2004) *Here, There and Everywhere*, Stoke-on-Trent: Trentham Books

Gillborn, D. and Ladson-Billings, G. (eds) (2004) *The Routledge Falmer Reader in Multicultural Education: critical perspectives on race, racism and education*, London: Routledge Falmer

Grant, C. and Sleeter, C. (2011) *Doing Multicultural Education for Achievement and Equity*, 2nd edn, London: Routledge

Hicks, D. and Holden, C. (2007) *Teaching and the Global Dimension*, London: Routledge

Higgins, S. (2009) 'Developing the global dimension in primary schools', *Policy & Practice: A Development Education Review*, 9, 52–8

McCabe, L. (1997) 'Global perspective development', *Education*, 118

Quality Curriculum Authority (QCA) (2007) *The Global Dimension in Action: a curriculum planning guide for schools*, London: Crown Printers

Oxfam (2007) *Global Citizenship Guides: building successful school partnerships* available at: http://www.oxfam.org.uk/education/ teachersupport/cpd/

Pickford, T. (ed.) (2009) *Get Global! A Practical Guide to Integrating the Global Dimension into the Primary Classroom*, Stoke on Trent: Trentham Books

Regan. C. (ed.) (2006) *80:20, Development in an Unequal World*, Bray: Educating and Acting for a Better World

Teachers in Development Education (TIDE) (2005) *Climate Change – Local and Global: an enquiry approach*, Birmingham: TIDE

Young, M. (2002) *Global Citizenship: the handbook for primary teaching*, Cambridge: Chris Kington Publishing

# What makes stereotypes pernicious? 23

### Stephen Scoffham

'Does your family carry a gun?' 'Is it foggy where you are? These were the two questions most frequently asked in an email exchange between eight-year-old children in London and Los Angeles, California, reported in a national newspaper (Shaw, 2003). No prizes for spotting the stereotype – we can all recognize them when we see them and we come across them all the time.

Stereotypes are generalizations that, while they may not be entirely accurate, contain an element of truth. They are usually applied to groups of people but they can also be applied to places or things. Some stereotypes are positive and emphasize good things. More often than not they have negative connotations. There is also a sense in which stereotypes operate as unthinking, kneejerk reactions. They tend to be unsophisticated and depend on caricature for their impact and effect.

The term stereotype was first coined nearly a century ago in 1922 by a social scientist, Walter Lippmann. Lippmann noted that rather than inter-preting new information on its merits we sometimes generalize on the basis of our existing ideas. Lippmann talked about stereotypes as 'pictures in our heads' and he recognized that they were remarkably rigid. Although there has been much discussion about what stereotypes mean in detail, the term has proved so useful on a general level that it has entered into popular language.

*What stereotypes do you and the children you teach hold? Which are positive and which are negative? Are any neutral?*

Stereotypes can help us to order our ideas. Current ideas about thinking and learning have identified the importance of generalizing and metacog-nition. It is by seeking patterns and organizing our thoughts into categories and groups that we make sense of our experience. While the search for common characteristics is extremely helpful, the problem with stereotypes is that they lack criticality. In a sense this aligns stereotypes with emotional responses – both involve drawing on past experience and allow us to interpret new situations quickly and efficiently. However, the problem with intellectual shortcuts of this kind is that can be misleading.

One area where stereotypes are particularly evident is in our ideas about other countries. Palmer and Birch (2005) report how word association tests with primary school children reveal that their perception of Africa is dominated by exotic and colourful images such as 'wild animals', 'jungles' and 'witch doctors'. It is all too easy for such images to become joined together in what the Nigerian writer Chimamanda Adichie calls 'a single story' (Adichie, 2009). Once formed, such stories tend to colour our thinking and attitudes to other people. All too often they lead us to deny the similarities between people and undermine our common humanity.

*Can you think of a negative stereotype that you once held about a country but which you have now abandoned? What caused your ideas to change?*

Stereotypes develop from an early age. It appears there are a number of processes involved:

- Social. Tajfel (1981) argues that young children absorb attitudes and prejudices about other people and nations well before they have any factual information about them. He explains that they actively seek information that conforms to the norms of the 'in' and 'out' groups of their surrounding culture as they seek to build their identity.
- Developmental. There are suggestions that pupils' ideas about the wider world depend on their developmental stage. While very young children tend to focus on their immediate surroundings, by the middle primary years they become more interested in the wider world. Their fear of the unknown colours their understanding and they start to relish stories of hunter-gatherers. Stereotypes from film and advertising tend to compound and distort these images still further.
- Cultural. Over the past few decades Edward Said (1993) and others have drawn attention to the notion of 'otherness' which equates difference in culture with distance in time. According to this interpretation, the more 'different' people are to 'us' the more they are living in the past. Thus when we describe a place as 'basic' or 'simple' we are tapping, either consciously or unconsciously into euro-centric, postcolonial stereotypes.

These considerations suggest that stereotypes are much more complex than they seem at first sight. They involve social, cultural, developmental and political dimensions. They appear to have a role to play in learning and operate on both a conscious and an unconscious level. Understanding how stereotypes operate requires an appreciation of both learning theory and child development.

*Take one negative stereotype that some children hold and consider how it might have evolved.*

Negative stereotypes can be particularly pernicious and underpin many of the conflicts between different groups of people both within and between countries. It is the teacher's responsibility to challenge negative stereotypes and to seek to present children with up-to-date and realistic images of different people and places. One way of doing this is to avoid generalizations and to focus on specific individuals and instances. Another is to present a range of images that complement and qualify each other. A third is to focus on similarities between people rather than their differences.

*In the context of a negative stereotype, what strategies would you use to alter children's perception?*

Wherever you are teaching, you are bound to hear children voicing negative stereotypes from time to time. It may be tempting to ignore them but they need to be challenged, either at the time or in a more measured manner at some later date. As Young puts it: 'If you intend to promote equality and fairness it is essential that you are aware of, and can tackle, any discriminatory views that pupils may express' (2005, p. 22). It's harder than it sounds but it's worth the effort.

# References and further reading

Adichie, C. (2009) 'The dangers of a single story' paper given at *TED Global*, available at: http:\\www.youtube.com/watch?v=D9Ihs241zeg (accessed September 2011)

Disney, A. (2005) 'Children's images of a distant locality', *International Research in Geography and Environmental Education*, 14:4, 330–35

Palmer, J. and Birch, J. (2005) *Geography in the Early Years*, London: Routledge

Said, E. (1993) *Culture and Imperialism*, London: Chatto & Windus

Scoffham, S. and Potter, C. (2007) 'Please miss, why are they so poor?', *Primary Geographer*, 62, 5–7

Shaw, M. (2003) 'E it's foggy in London town', *Times Educational Supplement*, 22 August

Tajfel, H. (1981) *Human Groups and Social Categories*, Cambridge: Cambridge University Press

Young, M. (2005) 'The global dimension', in Scoffham, S. (ed.) *Primary Geography Handbook*, Sheffield: Geographical Association

# 24 Should we teach children about current affairs?

## Stephen Scoffham

One primary school topic that often proves particularly successful is a project on the news and current affairs. Events that are happening around the world impinge on our lives in many subtle ways. Children are often aware of what is going on and appreciate the chance to find out more. They also welcome the opportunity to contribute items to a news noticeboard and to bring things from home into the classroom. The problem is that many news items raise complex issues and deal with distressing situations for which there are no easy answers.

*Think back over the key news stories from the last few months and consider the different dimensions involved.*

Some of the most dramatic news stories are to do with disasters. Volcanic eruptions, earthquakes, floods and famines often dominate the headlines. News reports and pictures from the internet capture what has happened with stunning accuracy. However, they can also be harrowing. One of the challenges for teachers is to tread the fine line between children's natural curiosity and the stark reality of conflicts and disasters.

Here are some possible constructive approaches to a news event about a hurricane:

- Find out some background knowledge and information. For example, find out about how they form and the tracks that they follow. As well as being interesting in its own right, this research can help to reassure pupils who may be anxious that their own home is in danger.
- Find out what people can do to protect themselves. For example, advance warning of floods and storms can help to save lives; dams, barriers and flood protection measures can help to reduce their impact.
- Find out about similar events in the past and speculate about what might happen in the future. This will capitalize on the children's interest and lead them towards a deeper level of understanding.

*Can you think of a constructive approach to a different disaster or event?*

One of the most natural responses to any disaster is to try to assist those affected. Schools have a long tradition of fundraising for charitable causes and do a great deal of very worthwhile work in this area. However, you also need to question what pupils learn from such activities and be alert to any hidden messages about power and dependency they may absorb, particularly if the focus is on the developing world. Martin (2010) reminds us that it is all too easy to slip into binary thinking that emphasizes the divisions between 'us' and 'them', 'poor' and 'wealthy', 'backward' and 'advanced'. Such views can lead to an unspoken assumption of superiority, which, when compounded by guilt about differences in wealth in a postcolonial world, make an unfortunate mix. Exploring the longer term causes of poverty and establishing direct links with schools overseas are two ways of mitigating these effects.

*Consider your own experience of school fundraising events as you reflect on these questions.*

One of the other principles to keep firmly in mind when teaching about current affairs is to avoid portraying people as victims. Agency and self-determination are a fundamental part of what it means to be alive and we tend to resent being helped by others because it undermines us and seems patronising. In his review of history and geography teaching, Knight (1993) touches on this idea when he declares: 'At the heart of any worthwhile work on other cultures is the fundamental, absolutely pervasive notion that people are human wherever they live which means that they make what seem to them to be intelligent decisions' (p. 71). This is a valuable starting point and we would do well to keep it firmly in mind in any exploration of current affairs.

In addition to natural disasters, news reports often feature environmental problems. Indeed, species loss, global warming and environmental degradation are seldom far from the public gaze. As well as involving complex processes, such issues also raise profound social and political questions. How can we explore these troubling matters without falling into denial or despair? One answer is to develop a sense of hope and optimism. This isn't to suggest a bland or vacuous frame of mind, rather the empowerment that comes from critical and creative engagement with real-life issues. As Hicks (2002) roundly declares: 'No problem, environmental or otherwise, should be taught about at any level in education without concomitant emphasis on strategies for its resolution' (p. 76). By adopting such an approach we can avoid turning our pupils into victims.

*With this approach in mind, how would you teach about a single environmental issue?*

Teachers tend to be wary of engaging with controversial issues. Such studies have the potential to lead to uncharted territory. They challenge us to clarify our own position and assumptions. There is also a danger that we will adopt a partisan approach – after all children don't come to school to be indoctrinated or to listen to propaganda. Yet there is no point in trying to pretend that children are unaware of real-world problems. From the five year old who is busy selling raffle tickets to 'save the polar bear', to the child who lies awake at night worrying about climate change, global issues permeate modern life. You might come to the conclusion that these matters do not constitute legitimate subject matter for the school curriculum. Perhaps there simply isn't time for them. Alternatively, you might decide that being well informed about such issues is a fundamental part of educating children for the future. Whatever you decide, you need to have thought about your position in some depth so you know how to respond to events as and when they occur.

# References and further reading

Hicks, D. (2002) *Lessons for the Future*, Oxford: Trafford

Knight, P. (1993) *Primary History, Primary Geography*, London: Fulton

Martin, F. (2010) 'Global ethics, sustainability and partnership', in Butt, G. (ed.), *Geography, Education and the Future*, London: Continuum

# Maps are increasingly being used by children but do these maps tell the truth?

Terry Whyte

The growth and easy availability of ICT has enabled the map to form a very popular part of everybody's lives in the last few years with the use of programs such as Google Earth, devices such as satellite navigation systems and mobile phone technology. Children are increasingly becoming comfortable with the images seen on screen of their world in a way previous generations could only imagine. Not only can children use mapping devices to find their own home on a digital map they can also locate treasure in the outdoors with geo-caching activities, are able to follow a route in their parents car and go even further by traversing the earth and the solar system in a mix of maps and satellite images. When playing electronic games children plan routes to escape the 'baddies' or describe which trail to use in order to rescue a friend, plan whole towns, manage a farm or decide where Postman Pat should collect and deliver mail around Greendale.

Despite the recent technological developments the innate appeal for children and adults of conventional maps and map making can be witnessed when associated with pirates and treasure and in the use of maps in fiction taking the reader into imaginative worlds with characters such as Winnie the Pooh in the Hundred Acres Wood, the children in Narnia or Hobbits in Middle Earth.

Opportunities to engage with maps on a variety of levels, within formal education and, increasingly, within normal play, indicates that children do enjoy using maps. Research suggests that from an early age children have certain map-engagement skills that might be associated with a universal survival imprint that we all have (Blaut and Shea, 1974). In particular, Catling (2005) states that children have key mapping skills ranging from being sure about moving around familiar environments, being able to model imaginary and real situations and in using simple maps to identify features and to find their way about. Importantly for educators, it is suggested that children are able to appreciate the bird's eye view and have a growing awareness of the world as a whole from an early age (Catling, 2005). Wiegand (2006) argues that in addition to the popularity of maps they have never been more relevant to education, particularly when the use of maps is so widespread in everyday life. It should be obvious that maps appear within the geography curriculum but aspects of graphicacy can be seen in other subject areas such as science, mathematics and PE.

*What experiences can you remember from your childhood of using maps and how does it differ from the use of maps by today's children?*

If maps have become a more significant part of children's experience, we should next ask, what do maps tell us and are they expressing the truth or do they lie? Map makers attempt to create reality and our perception of the world has been built up over time through the images that cartographers create. We accept that the United Kingdom takes the shape that it does or Italy looks like a boot because of the way it has been represented on a map. It is only recently through space exploration that this carefully constructed view of the earth, measured and plotted over centuries, has been confirmed through satellite photography. But even these images are managed by people.

In representing any part of the globe, maps are going to have a difficulty in flattening something that is round. The important domains of maps; shape, area, distance and direction are going to be modified in some way in order to represent reality on a flat dimension. For example, with direction most people living in the northern hemisphere would expect to see north oriented at the top of the map; however, the world has no real orientation as it simply exists in space.

*Consider the images provided in atlases. What influences do you think are present here?*

Local street maps have all the pertinent information of distance, signage and direction but are the areas depicted as in reality? Using Google, if you compare the map and the photograph of an area you will see how the mapmaker has selected information to represent on the map. Maps, perhaps, could be seen as being economical with the truth but is this to be seen as a deception? Maps are not objective miniature replicas of the world but are highly selective in what they show as well as in what they omit (Wiegand 2000). Maps can tell lies (Monmonier, 1996), but by omitting and selecting they can 'represent' the truth.

*Consider some of the maps drawn to represent single points such as population related to land area. How would you use these 'distorted' maps with children?*

Maps are created, for the most part, to express a version of reality but it does depend on what element of reality is being represented and for the reader who selects and chooses a map, for what purpose. We all expect certain conventions to be observed in the maps we read, use and indeed create ourselves. Places are usually dots of various sizes, roads and tracks coloured lines, water is blue and land is green. Because, on the whole, they are faithful, objective projections of some element of reality, the earth, we, as readers tend to trust them.

*How does this relate to children in working and understanding maps?*

Maps are powerful (Wood, 1992) and allow children to record and depict information about environments they know about and they begin to understand information about parts of their world that they will not be able to experience directly. Maps develop a sense of place locally and globally and can form opinions of their world from the past to the present and into the future (see Figure 25.1).

**Figure 25.1**

Does this image represent a child's view of their world, with their own conventions created, their own decisions on what to represent as the truth or is what we see a lie?

# References and further reading

Blaut, J. and Shea, D. (1974) 'Mapping at the age of three', *Journal of Geography*, 73, 5–9

Catling, S. (2005) 'Developing children's understanding and use of maps', in Lee, C. and Hung, C. (eds) *Primary Social Studies: exploring pedagogy and content*, Singapore: Marshall Cavendish Education

Lee, C. and Hung, C. (eds) *Primary Social Studies: exploring pedagogy and content*, Singapore: Marshall Cavendish Education

Monmonier, M. (1996) *How to Lie with Maps*, 2nd edn, Chicago: University of Chicago Press

Wiegand, P. (2006) *Learning and Teaching with Maps*, London: Routledge

Wood, D. (1992) *The Power of Maps*, New York: Guilford Press

[*Note*: download Google Earth internet. Any atlases and maps are useful tools.]

# Part IV
## Teachers' Professional Status

26  What are some philosophical, sociological and psychological
    perspectives on education?                                     109
27  What is meant by professional identity?                        113
28  What does professionalism mean for a teacher?                  117
29  Why should teachers be researchers?                            121
30  How do we improve our own practice?                            125
31  How can mentors and mentees make the most of the
    mentoring process?                                             128

Nothing in education is neutral and this includes each individual's approach to the way she teaches. Teachers are influenced by their own schooling, their training, the schools in which they work, policy, public perception and the children themselves. This series of chapters asks questions about how you view education and your own role within it. By reflecting on and exploring their own practice, teachers establish their identity and beliefs, which, in turn, underpin their decisions and actions in the classroom. And, finally, how do teachers influence the beliefs of others?

# What are some philosophical, sociological and psychological perspectives on education? 26

Rosemary Walters

Bertrand Russell (1926) commented: 'We are faced with the paradoxical fact that education has become one of the chief obstacles to intelligence and freedom of thought' (p. 28). This is a serious allegation. We need to ask what would constitute evidence for this and could it be equally applied today? So ask yourself what is education providing for the children you teach? Do you feel it is equipping them with a sense of their physical, social, intellectual and cultural world? Is it transforming their lives? Will it get them a job? Alongside all the energy and dynamism invested in studying pedagogies of teaching and learning, it is important to consider education from other more esoteric perspectives. This chapter sets out to introduce three perspectives on education: the philosophical considering the nature and characteristics of education; the sociological considering how education is structured within society and for what purpose; and, finally, the psychological perspective considering how education relates to theories of human development.

*What do you see as the long-term effects of teaching the children in your class? Consider this question in the context of one of your pupils.*

The Latin definition of *educare* is to lead out. This requires examining in more depth to consider what is being led out, the qualities and training of the leaders and how far current practice is more accurately described as putting a curriculum in! Tibble (1966, p. 71) quotes the classic philosopher of education, Peters, as defining education as 'a family of processes concerned with the intentional transmission of something valuable in a morally unobjectionable manner'. The presumption here is that there is a body of content that has been classified as valuable and that there are acceptable ways of passing this on. The definition of valuable and acceptable in this context depends on viewpoints and must be open to debate.

*Who decides what is valuable and how it is transmitted?*

Tibble (1966, p. 79) uses another stimulating quote from Peters when he describes an educator as 'someone who initiates others into forms of thought and awareness which will transform their world and how they see it?' The term 'transformative education' is often used with approval and implies that the world of learner is in some way constantly renewed and opened to new perspectives through subjecting existing experience to fresh knowledge and understanding. The teacher must also be open to and aware of the potential and actual possibilities of transformation within their own learning journey alongside the learner and one of the purposes of reflective practice is to identify this.

*Is it important to make a connection between transformation and education? Have you seen transformation happening in classrooms?*

If we examine education from the view of the sociologist, we see a different picture. Swift (1969, p. 8) said: 'Education is the way in which we acquire the physical, moral and social capacities demanded by the group into which we are born and in which we shall function.'

Education also includes all teaching and learning that goes on in society, formal and informal, intended and unintended. However, society has decided it needs schools and therefore teachers to undertake a major part of the task of delivering education and, according to Swift:

> Modern society has set aside particular individuals with the special task (educating) to which they will devote a major part of their working energy and has established an occupational category of teacher. (1969, p. 9)

*Are there alternatives to this approach?*

Possibly modern industrial society is so complex that we need an organized method for preparing children for adult life and parents have neither the time nor the expertise to educate children effectively. In such a complex society, it seems strange that schools are relatively similar with static rather than fluid boundaries, for example the opportunity for parents or other adults to join in full time with children's education is rare. Usher and Edwards (1994) argue that education is an aspect of living for everyone and therefore there is no place for categories such as elitist. What should schools be designed to achieve: cultured and emotionally intelligent people, knowledgeable people, employable people, equality of opportunity, social mobility, or perhaps a combination of all of these? Depending on the balance of these elements schools have the capacity to reproduce and/or change society.

*What do you consider the purpose of the primary school?*

In return for the investment that society makes in schools, teachers are required to preserve the culture of their society (itself an interesting point given the global context of many local communities), promote economic development (for the many, the few?) and produce good citizens (as defined by whom?) (see Winch and Gingell, 1999; Bartlett et al., 2001) It is not surprising that many competing pressure groups expect to have a finger in the pie of educational decisions. The government, parents, employers, teachers and local communities all feel the right and need to comment on curriculum, behaviour and organizational matters.

*Who do you see as having the greatest influence on education?*

In considering education from a psychology perspective, Kernig (1989) highlights the perspective of Susan Isaacs in *The Children We Teach* (1932), that the children, in particular their character and development, must be the priority in the enterprise of teaching. The selection and outcome of teaching methods must relate to the successful learning and understanding of the child in addition to their physical growth and social needs.

Every teacher is searching for the key to good relationships between adults and other adults and adults and children within the classroom. And the key to good relationships is an understanding of one's self as an important element of understanding others. Morris argues that the teacher 'should be a major resource for making and sustaining fruitful relationships between children and children and children and adults by defending the integrity of each individual's personality' (Morris in Tibble, 1966, p. 171).

There may be difficulties for the teacher in the defence of less conformist or more hostile personalities but Morris holds out this integrity as a non-negotiable element in the working out of behaviour management.

Teachers are faced with two crucial tensions that need resolving. In delivering the content of the curriculum, there may be tension between intellectual objectivity and moral conviction within some subject matter. In behaviour management, the teacher has to strike a balance between detachment and sympathetic understanding of each individual pupil.

*Is there a conflict between behaviour management and defending the integrity of the individual child's personality?*

# References and further reading

Bartlett, S. Burton, D. and Piem, N. (2001) *Introduction to Education Studies*, London: Paul Chapman

Isaacs, S. (1932) *The Children We Teach*, London: University of London Press

Kernig, W. (1989) 'Research into the effectiveness of primary education in England and Wales: a historical perspective', *Early Child Development and Care*, 44:1

Richards, C. (2006) 'Primary teaching: a personal perspective', in Arthur, J., Grainger, T. and Wray, D. (2006) *Learning to Teach in the Primary School*, London: Routledge

Russell, B. (1926) *Theory of Knowledge*, Encyclopedia Britannica, 13th edn

Swift, D. (1969) *The Sociology of Education*, London: Routledge & Kegan Paul

Tibble, J. (ed.) (1966) *The Study of Education*, London: Routledge & Kegan Paul

Usher, R. and Edwards, R. (1994) *Postmodernism and Education*, London: Routledge

Winch, C. and Gingell, J. (1999) *Key Concepts in the Philosophy of Education*, London: Routledge

# What is meant by professional identity?

## Vanessa Young

## 27

When you decided to become a teacher, it is likely that you had a very particular idea of what kind of teacher you wanted to be.

*List four qualities/strengths that you feel you possess as a teacher and two that you aspire to. You may wish to discuss and compare your list with a colleague.*

All teachers need to have a clear sense of who they are as professionals. They need to ask themselves the question: who am I as a teacher? What kind of teacher do I want to become? The notion of identity implies self-knowledge: knowledge of what we believe and why, what we value, what motivates us, how we learn and where we stand on key issues. This identity will have been shaped and influenced by our background and upbringing, our class, culture, ethnicity and religion. Our experiences, also, will have a bearing on our professional identity as will our key attributes and will influence how we see ourselves as teachers and ultimately how we behave. If you are a good listener for example, this might lead you to place a particular value on communication and the importance of 'pupil voice'. If you are an imaginative, creative person, you are more likely to emphasize open-ended, problem-solving approaches in your classroom. Personal and professional identities are inextricably linked in this way. Our professional identity will impact on our views about learning, our teaching style, our approach to the curriculum – indeed, our whole educational ideology.

*What aspects of your personal identity impact on your professional identity? What external factors have helped to shape your sense of professional identity?*

Thinking consciously about who you are can promote resilience in a stressful profession (Forde et al., 2006, in McMahon et al., 2011). It can help to develop motivation and confidence and clarify your professional goals. In times of constant change, especially when there is a radical shift in political educational policy, a clearer sense of identity will help teachers to know how to think about and respond to new initiatives – not simply as an implementer or deliverer, but as someone who professionally critiques, shapes and develops them, applying their knowledge and understanding about how children learn.

It is important, however, to realize that identity is not something fixed; it is not a static 'state', but something that develops over the course of one's entire life (Erikson, in Beijaard et al., 2004). Mead used the concept of identity in relationship with the concept of 'self'. This sounds on the face of it, a personal, introspective process, but 'the self' is always mediated by the environment; it exists in a social setting where there is social communication; in communicating we learn to assume the roles of others and monitor our actions accordingly (Beijaard et al., 2004). This is significant for us in teaching as it suggests that our interactions with other stakeholders, including teachers, parents and of course the children will be paramount in helping to shape who we are and who we become as professionals. It can feel uncomfortable – especially if our existing thinking and 'pet theories' are challenged and we find ourselves pushed into new ways of working and thinking. This is all a healthy part of the process of developing identity. What can appear negative can ultimately have very positive outcomes.

Recently, the whole notion of professionalism has become much more aligned with government policy (England). We have become a much more 'managed' profession (Furlong, 2008, in McMahon et al., 2011). This is not that new. Back in 1995, Helsby observed that:

> The current structures for teacher education would not seem tailored to support the necessary development of critical capacities, reflective practice or a meaningful interchange with colleagues to agree a shared set of values and professional knowledge; rather they seem organized to facilitate uncritical implementation of government policies, casting the teacher in the role of 'agent of the National Curriculum'. (p. 329)

This kind of 'managerialism' tends to construct professionalism in terms of compliance and conformity (Forde et al., 2006, in McMahon et al., 2011). The more that autonomy is tied up with a teacher's sense of their own professional identity (as has tended to be the case in England), the more they will feel uncomfortable about being managed in this way. This shift in culture then presents challenges in terms of professional identity. Consider these two positions:

Scenario 1: Teacher A has a very strong sense of her own personal identity. She knows what she believes and these values permeate and guide all her professional actions. She is often heard to say 'that's the kind of teacher I am ...' or 'that's the way we do it in my class ...'. She is highly resistant to any idea that is new or different, even in the face of convincing evidence.

Scenario 2: Teacher B has a very unclear sense of his own professional identity. As a result, he often feels anxious and finds it hard to make professional decisions. He often changes his mind mid-stream. He always thinks other people's ideas are better than his and therefore tries to implement, uncritically, any new initiative that comes along.

Shain and Gleeson characterized teacher responses to the increasingly managerial culture as showing: 'rejection and resistance, compliance or strategic compliance' (in Lawy and Tedder, 2011). Neither of these positions is desirable in terms of professional identity. The issue here is not just about resistance or acceptance, but rather that neither Teacher A nor Teacher B is reflecting thoughtfully and critically.

The dynamic process of developing one's professional identity requires continuous and deliberate examination and nurturing. The teacher does not emerge from initial training or even professional development as 'the finished article', but rather as someone who has learned to be in a continuous state of learning – not just on technical aspects, but on bigger questions such as: 'What should the aims of primary education be?' Even the most proficient of practitioners will find themselves shuttling continuously back and forwards between confidence and self-doubt (Colley et al., 2007, in McMahon et al., 2011). Self-doubt can arise from taking on a new role where one's expertise is not so well developed; or it can simply be the result of a bad lesson or the inability to get through to a particular child. The reflective practitioner, does not view these 'set-backs' negatively, but rather sees them as an opportunity for enquiry and subsequent growth.

*Identify when moments of self-doubt and confidence have occurred for you. How have you capitalized on these to promote your own learning?*

The teacher as professional therefore needs to be engaged in what Schön (1983) refers to as 'reflection-in-action'. Handscomb and MacBeath (2003) refer to this as 'teacher as enquirer'. This places teachers in a very different relationship with not only their own practice, but also with government policy. Teachers are not merely deliverers of the curriculum; they develop it, refine it and interpret it too (Hargreaves and Fullan, 1992). This is key to the development of a strong and effective professional identity.

*What do you do to systematically reflect on your action in the classroom?*

# References and further reading

Beijaard, D., Meijer, P. and Verloop, N. (2004) 'Reconsidering research on teachers' professional identity', *Teaching and Teacher Education*, 20, 107–28

Handscomb, G. and MacBeath, J. (2003) *The Research-engaged School*, Colchester, Essex County Council: FLARE

Hargreaves, A. and Fullan, M. (1992) *Understanding Teacher Development*, New York: Cassell

Helsby, G. (1995) 'Teachers' construction of professionalism in England in the 1990s', *Journal of Education for Teaching*, 21:3, 317–31

Lawy, R. and Tedder, M. (2011) 'Beyond compliance: teacher education practice in a performative framework', *Research Papers in Education* available at: http\\www.ioe.stir.ac.ukpp445-462 (accessed October 2011)

McMahon, M., Forde, C. and Martin, M. (2011) *Contemporary Issues in Learning and Teaching*, London: Sage

Schön, D. (1983) *The Reflective Practitioner: how professionals think in action*, London: Temple Smith

# What does professionalism mean for a teacher?

## 28

### Peter Dorman

How do we understand and describe the features of teaching as a profession? Jacques and Hyland (2007) provide what appears to be a clear outline. They suggest that professions are marked by the following characteristics:

- 'possession of specialized knowledge and skills, successful completion of intellectual and practical education and training
- conformity to ethical standards when dealing with clients commitment to the competence and integrity of the professional as a whole; membership of an organized body involved in testing competence and regulating competence and conduct.' (p. 202)

Whilst such a clear-cut set of descriptors may at first appear helpful it could also be argued that they are so general in nature that they could as easily applied to almost any other work-related activity. Surely it could be argued that an electrician or plumber can just as equally claim professionalism in line with these criteria? It is perhaps the ease that we talk about the importance for teachers to act, and to be seen by the government and the wider public, as professionals, without actually specifying the nature of that professionalism that lies at the heart of the current debate.

*What is your understanding of teacher as professional?*

The criteria suggested reflect the earlier work of Millerson (1964) who wrote at the start of the Plowden era and at a time when the nature of teacher professionalism seemed more certain, though whether this certainty was actual or is simply a comforting myth has been and should be questioned (Alexander, 2007). What is perhaps more certain is that in the intervening years the nature of teacher professionalism has become an area of intense debate. This debate has been sustained from Prime Minister James Callaghan's famous speech at Ruskin College in 1976, through the Conservative years of National Curriculum development and implementation in the 1980s and 1990s, into the New Labour years, which saw perhaps the most explicit attempt to redesign and credentialise teacher professionalism.

Writing at the start of the millennium, Hargreaves and Lo (2000) described teaching as a 'paradoxical, perhaps a uniquely paradoxical profession' (p. 68). They suggest that at a time when teaching is 'charged with the formidable task of creating the human skills and capacities that will enable societies to survive and succeed in the age of information', the profession becomes one of the 'first casualties of the slimmed-down state that informational societies and their economies seem to require'. They further suggest that 'just when the very most is expected of them, teachers appear to be being given less support, less respect, and less opportunity to be creative, flexible and innovative than before' (p. 1). And, at the time of writing, the new coalition government is set to continue this process with renewed intensity. Changes to school structures, terms and conditions of employment and the development of a new curriculum with, in part at least, a prescribed teaching pedagogy are examples under consideration. This brief history gives a background to the continued debate about the meaning of professional in a teaching context.

More recently, a report authored jointly by the independent think tank DEMOS and the General Teaching Council (Craig and Fieschi, 2007) begins:

> Ask a politician about teachers and they will tell you about schools – ask a teacher about themselves and they will tell you about their pupils. Teacher professionalism is inextricably linked to 'what is best for children', this is the end of teacher professionalism, it is both the motivation and the desired outcome. (p. 2)

The authors then move beyond this static position of simply describing 'teacher professionalism' to argue that, if teaching is actually about, 'doing the best for children', it is to examine the type of professional who is needed in the coming years. They propose the development of what they term 'DIY professionalism', that is a form of professionalism constructed by individuals and teams of individuals in light of their local circumstances and concerns. Their proposal may seem at first a radical suggestion as it fragments the unified and shared understanding of teacher professionalism but it may be that there is such a shared view is in itself a further myth.

*To better understand the argument, try this exercise. First, ask yourself the seemingly simple question, 'What is best for children?' Having done this, ask other colleagues, of both genders, of differing educational backgrounds, ages and levels of teaching experience how they would answer the question. Perhaps the overlaps and, importantly, the differences in their answers may help you to understand the authors' argument.*

More recently research at the University of Cambridge (Swann et al., 2010) has examined teachers' own conceptions of what it means to be a professional. The research used two large-scale surveys in 2003 and again in 2006. As you may find when discussing the term teacher professionalism with friends and colleagues, there is not one single integrated view of professionalism. Rather they hold a central core of shared beliefs and commitments. These are comprised of two elements:

1 an assertion and celebration of the expertise needed to do the complicated job of classroom teaching
2 a desire for the profession to be more widely trusted by the government and the general public.

The report further suggests that this final point may reflect what Whitty (2002) described as the development of a 'low-trust' relationship between society and its teachers that was encouraged then belatedly, if half-heartedly, recognized by New Labour (Swann et al., 2010, p. 567).

The research also notes that beyond the established central core of beliefs lies a range of further and more contested factors. They note, for example, that teachers being involved in research, is very far from being accepted as a core element of teacher professionalism and that teaching requires collaboration with others, which they link to the previous administration's 'widening participation agenda', is not universally seen as a part of the central core of shared beliefs.

*Do you see these two aspects of being a teacher as important and why?*

The ongoing contested nature of teacher professionalism is further reflected in the work of Warin et al. (2006), in particular, the manner in which personal and professional views of teacher professionalism may conflict. Reflecting Piagetian principles, they term this conflict 'identity dissonance', that feeling we have when we realise that what we consider to be core values and beliefs are not held in common by colleagues.

*Discuss with colleagues how you see your professional identity.*

# References and further reading

Alexander, R. (2007) 'Where there is no vision', *Symposium Journals* available at: http://www.primaryreview.org.uk/Downloads/PDFs/19_Alexander_FORUM_49_1_2.pdf (accessed September 2011)

Craig, J. and Fieschi, C. (2007) 'DIY professionalism: futures for teaching', Demos in association with GTC available at: http://www.demos.co.uk/files/ DIY%20Professionalism.pdf (accessed September 2011)

Hargreaves, A. and Lo, L. (2000) 'The parodical profession: teaching at the turn of the century', *Prospect*, 30:2

Jacques, K. and Hyland, R. (2007) *Professional Studies: primary and early years*, Exeter: Learning Matters

Millerson, G. (1964) *The Qualifying Associations: a study in professionalization*, London: Routledge & Kegan Paul

Swann, M., McIntyre, D., Pell, T., Hargreaves, L. and Cunningham, M. (2010) 'Teachers', *British Educational Research Journal*, 36:23

Warin, J., Maddock, M., Pell, A. and Hargreaves, L. (2006) 'Resolving identity dissonance through reflective and reflexive practice in teaching', *Reflective Practice*, 7, 233–45

Whitty, G. (2002) 'Why teachers matter: policy agendas and social trends', in *Teachers Matter*, Maidenhead: McGraw-Hill/Open University Press

# Why should teachers be researchers? 29
### Viv Wilson

In order to consider this question, we first have to think about what we mean by the word 'research'. Some people find the idea of research off-putting, and assume it means having to undertake time-consuming study involving statistics or large-scale surveys and that it has little relevance to everyday classroom practice (McNamara, 2002). Educational research of this type is certainly carried out, more usually by specialist research organizations such as National Foundation for Educational Research or by university-based researchers, but it isn't the only kind of research worth considering – neither is it always disconnected with classroom practice.

*What does the word 'research' mean to you?*

However it is carried out, research seeks to develop new knowledge and understanding whether this is new to you as an individual or to a wider audience. Whatever research method is used, researchers collect their evidence systematically and seek to analyse it with as open a mind as possible. Researchers aim to link their findings with other research and knowledge and to share their findings with others. Many teachers say that they don't have the time to 'do research on top of teaching', perhaps because they feel that 'research' is something separate from their everyday work. Conversely, though, it could be argued that investigating learning is both a form of research and also an essential part of teaching.

*How do you see yourself as a researcher? What would you choose to know more about in your classroom either about your teaching or the children's learning?*

The idea of the teacher-as-researcher has been well established in the United Kingdom for many years, influenced by the work of Lawrence Stenhouse (1975). Stenhouse argued that good teachers needed to be autonomous in their professional judgement and that this could only happen if they were actively examining, and experimenting with their own teaching. 'The uniqueness of each classroom setting implies that any proposal – even at school level – needs to be tested and verified and adapted by each teacher in his [sic] own classroom' (op. cit., p. 143).

It could be argued, though, that teachers no longer need to develop their own teaching ideas. The development of centralized guidance documents on curriculum, and teaching and learning, such as those from the previous National Strategies, and the criteria from OFSTED on good practice tell us clearly what we should be teaching and how we should teach it.

*Do you think the role of teacher as researcher is still appropriate and, if yes, why?*

The response to this question depends on your view of the teacher as a professional. If your view is that professional teachers are those who are able to make their own judgements about teaching and learning, based on critical evaluation of evidence, then you are likely to see school-based research as an important part of this process. This can be challenging in the face of well-established centralised directives and perhaps a culture operating within the school that makes questioning accepted practice difficult. The new Standards for Teachers, which apply from September 2012, imply that a critical and questioning atttitude is expected of all teachers and that they should 'demonstrate a critical understanding of developments in the subject and curriculum areas, and promote the value of scholarship' (TDA, 2011). This standard reflects some aspects of the research process, such as critical analysis and considering theory.

There is plenty of evidence to suggest that where teachers do adopt a questioning approach, and especially where they work together, they can make a clear difference to pupils' learning and achievement through systematic investigation of aspects of teaching and learning (Cordingley et al., 2003; Durrant and Holden 2006). Every initiative needs adapting for the particular children in a school and your classes, whether it comes from government guidance, a staff training course or teachers' own reading.

*Have you followed a line of enquiry that has made a difference to the way you work?*

The most commonly used term to describe teachers' research is that of 'action research': 'Action research is trying out an idea in practice with a view to improving or changing something, trying to have a real effect on the situation' (Kemmis, 1981, p. 8).

Action research is often described as a spiral or cyclical process in which the teacher-researcher(s) plan a change to practice, implement it, evaluate it in some way and reflect on the result. Further actions are based on what has been learned and the spiral continues. Cordingley et al. (2003) found that where teachers adopted this type of approach and worked together, they were able to sustain new ideas and embed them in practice, leading to clear improvements in pupils' learning and achievement.

In order to do this, teachers need to be systematic in collecting and examining evidence of the impact of the changes they are introducing. This can take a number of forms, including observation, analysis of pupils' work, tape recording, interviews with colleagues or pupils to name but a few. Collecting this information, analysing it carefully and reflecting on the results provides evidence that helps to embed change and convince others of its value.

Some people argue that action research isn't 'proper research' because it is too small scale and unlikely to be objective because the teacher-researchers are too close to the situation they are examining to be able to analyse it properly. They also suggest that a teacher research cannot add to new knowledge because their research cannot be generalized. That is, since each classroom or school is unique, it cannot be assumed that what happens in one place will automaticallly happen in another. While there is some truth in these views, they also depend on people's ideas about what research is. It could also be argued that the results of large-scale research investigations are so general that they cannot be applied to individual schools or classrooms without adaptation – which is exactly where teacher-research activity becomes important!

*What research carried out by others, small or large scale, have you used in your practice?*

Why should you be a researcher? There are different ways to answer this question, but the key point that emerges is this: teachers should be researchers in order to improve the quality of teaching and learning in their schools and classrooms. Through school-based research, teachers understand their pupils better and are able to identify more effective ways to support their learning.

# References and further reading

Cordingley, P., Bell, M., Rundell, B. and Evans, D. (2003) 'The impact of collaborative CPD on classroom teaching and learning', *Research Evidence in Education Library*, London: EPPI-Centre, Social Science Research Unit, Institute of Education, University of London

Durrant, J. and Holden, G. (2006) *Teachers Leading Change: doing research for school improvement*, London: Paul Chapman

Hopkins, D. (2002) *A Teacher's Guide to Classroom Research*, Maidenhead: Open University Press

Kemmis, S. (ed.) (1981) *The Action Research Reader*, Geelong: Deakin University Press

McNamara, O. (ed.) (2002) *Becoming an Evidence Based Practitioner*, London: Routledge Falmer

Stenhouse, L. (1975) *An Introduction to Curriculum Research and Development*, London: Heinemann

Thomas, G. (2009) *How to do Your Research Project*, London: SageTraining and Development Agency

(TDA) (2011) *Draft Standards for Teachers*, London: TDA; available at: www.tda.gov.uk

# How do we improve our own practice? 30

## Viv Wilson

In a previous chapter, we discussed whether teachers should be researchers, and saw that there is evidence to suggest that adopting a systematic approach to implementing and evaluating curriculum innovation or to developing new approaches to teaching and learning, can contribute to whole school improvement. We also argued that an important part of being a professional is to exercise critical judgement on aspects of practice. A natural extension of these points would be to apply these principles to our own classroom. It is common practice to evaluate aspects of our own teaching and children's learning. It is less common for teachers to undertake research style investigation.

*What is the value of reflecting on our own practice and researching in our own classrooms? Can the result of investigating our own practice be shared with other people, or is it just too 'subjective' or 'biased' to be of any use?*

Are research and reflection/evaluation the same? While they employ several common skills such as observation, recording, decision making and subsequent action, one difference is that the outcomes of reflection tend to be aimed at relatively short-term and often very specific ends. For example, you may have identified a particular aspect of a lesson that needs reviewing before the class can move on to the next topic.

A research investigation into an aspect of classroom practice would normally focus on a slightly broader issue and be conducted over a longer period of time. Most crucially, the investigation would be planned and systematic: you would decide on a particular approach that you believe would resolve an issue you had identified, you would monitor your progress and evaluate the outcome in an appropriate way. Thus classroom research is more formalised than reflection on learning, although it would usually develop from your reflection in some way.

In a research approach, Elliot (1991) emphasizes the importance of 'reconnaissance' before developing a plan of action and putting it into practice. This initial period of fact finding and analysis is crucial to the success of the investigation. Your first idea may be based on reflection on or evaluation of your teaching, on evidence from assessment of pupils' work and/or on observation of pupils' engagement with learning in certain situations or (most probably) on several types of evidence. This first idea may change and develop as you begin to investigate further:

> Be aware that the research question might change as you develop the research. The question 'How do I help my students concentrate?' might transform into the question 'How do I make my lessons more interesting so that my students want to learn?' As you reveal issues through studying your practice you will come to new understandings about yourself and the problematics of your situation and begin asking new questions. (McNiff and Whitehead, 2002, p. 86)

Your focus does not need to be on 'putting something right'. An equally valid reason for engaging in an investigation would be to introduce a new idea or approach to your teaching, even where no 'problem' is evident.

*Have you conducted research in your teaching? Do you have an area that you would like to investigate in more depth?*

The new Standards for Teachers (TDA, 2011) encourage us to 'promote the value of scholarship', which is generally defined as 'knowledge obtained by study'. While we have a responsibility to promote this with our pupils, we should also be seeing this as part of our own professional learning and development and there is a wealth of literature available that can help us understand the outcomes of our own classroom investigations better. Some of it is about how to carry out research in schools but there is also material about the results of other people's research that might inform our own practice.

It would seem that some teachers do not always see the value of reading other people's research, unless it provides ideas they can put directly into practice. Not all educational research sets out to provide such ideas, but this does not mean it is not relevant to classroom practice in other ways. Reading other people's ideas can help us think differently about why we do what we do, as well as providing ideas about how to do it.

Some definitions of what it means to be an education professional include the ability to examine one's work as a teacher in the wider social context and to ask questions about why we do things as we do (e.g. Hoyle, 1980). Reading educational literature, including research, and reflecting on our own practice can support this type of questioning – although it may not provide definite answers!

*Consider whether research should provide definite answers to some of these questions.*

There is a huge amount of material available that provides case studies and examples of practice that could help you to refine your own teaching and gives you ideas to test through systematic investigation in your own classroom. Some of these materials are written by teachers to share their own classroom-based research (website details are given later) and they offer a good response to the argument that classroom-based research is too 'subjective' to be of value to others.

'Reflexivity' is a term used to encourage people to consider how their own values and assumptions might affect the way they think about their approach to their development as a teacher and what they find out and can lead to increased self-awareness, although this might not always be comfortable. A possible value of reflecting and researching in our own classrooms is that it can help us understand ourselves better as teachers, as well as helping us understand learners and learning better.

Through analysis of our own actions and those of the pupils we can learn more about ourselves and our students and by linking this with ideas from other teachers and from research knowledge we become better able to make judgements based on evidence, and better able to justify our actions both to ourselves and to others. 'Teachers do not merely deliverer the curriculum. They develop, define it and reinterpret it too' (Dillon and Maguire, 2011).

# References and further reading

Dillon, J. and Maguire, M. (2011) *Developing as a Beginning Teacher* available at: http://www. mcgraw-hill.co.uk/openup/chapters/9780335221448.pdf (accessed October 2011)

Elliot, J. (1991) *Action Research for Educational Change*, Buckingham: Open University Press

Hoyle, E. (1980) 'Professionalization and de-professionalization in education', in Hoyle, E. and Megarry, J. (eds) *World Yearbook of Education 1980: the professional development of teachers*, London: Kogan Page

McNiff, J. with Whitehead, J. (2002) *Action Research: principles and practice*, 2nd edn, London: Routledge Falmer

National Teacher Research Panel available at: http://www.ntrp.org.uk/ Teaching and Learning Research Programme available at: http://www.tlrp.org/who/ practitioner.html

Training and Development Agency (TDA) (2011) *Draft Standards for Teachers*, London: TDA; available at: www.tda.gov.uk

Wilson, E. (2009) School-Based Research: a guide for education students, London: Sage

Wilson, V. and Kendall-Seatter, S. (2010) 'Why investigate', *Developing Professional Practice 7–14* Harlow: Pearson

# How can mentors and mentees make the most of the mentoring process?

**31**

Donna Birrell

As trainees and teachers, you will be mentees and mentors at various points as you develop as a professional. Whether you are a new mentor or being mentored, understanding both sides of the process is crucial in ensuring all parties fulfil their maximum potential. This chapter aims to consider the process and outlines some effective approaches to being a mentor and being a mentee.

Regardless of whether you are a trainee, a newly qualified teacher (NQT) or an experienced teacher, the desirable qualities required of a mentee essentially remain unchanged. There is consensus that gaining the most as a mentee is about asking questions and undertaking enquiry. For Edwards and Collison (1996), this is about mentees seeing themselves as learners in the classroom and, for Claxton (1999), it is about regarding genuine confusion as being part of the learning process.

Within the literature regarding the important qualities of teachers, reflection features highly as an aspect that is essential and it also features as an integral part of the standards required of newly qualified and experienced teachers (Tang and Chow 2007). Philosopher Dewey back in1933 (cited in Furlong and Maynard, 1995) considered that true reflection occurs in teachers who are 'committed to open mindedness, responsibility and wholeheartedness' (p. 42).

*Consider Dewey's terms. Are they features you identify with when considering the term reflection?*

Claxton (1999) also thinks 'reflection' is crucial to teaching but uses this in conjunction with 'resilience' and 'resourcefulness'. These terms combined create what has become known as the '3Rs' (p. 326). Reflection for Claxton means being mindful, which for him enables a departure from routine in favour of enquiry. Maybe considering Claxton's 3Rs is easier to associate with and we can see that reflection is more than just remembering past events or facts.

*Consider the 3Rs and evaluate their value as a mentee.*

Furthermore, in the literature there is the notion that reflection can occur in stages. Furlong and Maynard (1995) outline the ideas of Ziechner and Liston who consider just this. They believe that at Level 1, student teachers function as technicians where they concentrate on the more practical issues. It is at Level 2 (teacher as craftsperson) and at Level 3 (teacher as moral craftsperson) where they believe questions and justifications are considered within wider contexts (p. 41). Therefore, in light of reflection occurring in stages, the ability to question one's practice is essential in order to progress through the levels. It is by playing an active role in dialogues that this can be achieved and, as stated previously, Claxton suggests that genuine confusion should reveal itself during such conversations. He believes that there is the perception that teachers are the 'fount of all knowledge' (p. 70) and it is because of this that revealing any signs of uncertainty is avoided by teachers. It is through such questioning that enquiry and learning can become integral parts of our own professional development.

*Consider your professional development. Do you think you have progressed in stages and can you describe these stages?*

To summarize, as a mentee, it is about what we do with our recall of facts in view of instigating change for ourselves. Such enquiry will instigate change at a 'meta level' (Holland, 1989, cited in Tang and Chow, 2007). It is about taking responsibility for our own learning and questioning what we do and why we do it.

Being a mentor is about facilitating the desirable qualities we want to see in our mentees. As highlighted earlier, these qualities are being open minded, revealing uncertainty, asking questions and instigating change as a result. It is therefore from knowing what we want to achieve in our mentees that we can tailor our approach to mentoring.

In the literature, there are many approaches to and interpretations of the role (Maynard and Furlong, 1993; Berliner, 1994). This, in turn, corresponds to the many situations that can occur within the journeys undertaken by mentees at different points of their development. It also becomes apparent that there is no rigid framework through which all mentors proceed, as mentoring does not exist within a vacuum. Mentors and mentees work within a social dimension where situations, personalities and other factors affect the process. If promoting reflective teacher practitioners or independent learners is a key aim, then mentoring is about resolving difficulties through consideration of how to achieve this (Calderhead, 1989).

*Think of one key attribute you would like to promote in your mentee? How might you achieve this?*

Let us take responsibility as an example. If a mentee is responsible, they take an active role in their own development, wanting to progress for themselves.

But alongside this, responsibility must also lie with the mentor in providing the environment in which this can happen (Jones, 2001). Before you tailor your programme to promote responsibility or any other attribute, you might like to consider the following:

- the stage your mentee is at in their development as a teacher or pupil
- any social and external factors that may affect the process
- the amount of support you should give and what the support should look like
- the situations where critical thinking can be promoted
- whether your approach to mentoring should remain static throughout the process?

A useful framework to consider initially would be the mentoring model adopted by Daloz (1986, cited in McIntyre et al., 1994). He suggests that if students are allowed to just find their own way and get on with the practicalities with little support, there is likely to be no growth in their development. Where there is a breakdown with a student's performance, the challenge for the student is often high, but the support given to them is probably low. Daloz believes that the support needed for professional growth has to remain high, even when the challenges and competencies of a student are also high. It is commonplace that once a mentee has demonstrated basic competence that mentors tend to withdraw and let the student/pupil get on with it (Tang and Chow 2007) and it is only when things break down that reflection is re-instigated. Elliot and Calderhead (McIntyre et al., 1994) hope that reflection can grow from positivity and not just when things go wrong. Other useful mentoring models to consider are those of Maynard and Furlong (Maynard and Furling 1993; Furling and Maynard 1995) and Berliner (1994).

Let us reconsider Dewey's 'open mindedness'. This is a quality desirable of mentees, but it can be argued that it is just as relevant for mentors. Being open and asking open questions within quality conversations is an essential part of the mentoring process. Open questioning encourages deeper understanding and justifications from the mentee, but Jones (2001) advocates that an effective relationship between mentor and mentee is essential if this is to succeed. Corbett and Wright (1990, cited in McIntyre et al., 1994) mirror the thoughts put forward by Jones (2001) and advise that partnerships be based on 'trust and non-judgmental interest, support and challenge' (p. 228).

*How would you facilitate an open conversation about a difficulty and how would you ensure a non-judgemental approach?*

To conclude, if there is always heavy emphasis on immediate classroom practice, personal aspects, enthusiasm and general commitment rather than on the transferral of knowledge to wider contexts, then the development of morals and beliefs will be limited (Tang, 2002, cited in Tang and Chow, 2007, pp. 1067–8). As a mentor, your approach will significantly affect the behaviour and potential of your mentee.

# References and further reading

Berliner, D. (1994) 'Teacher expertise', in Moon, B. and Shelton Mayes, L. (eds) *Teaching and Learning in the Secondary School*, London: Routledge

Calderhead, J. (1989) 'Reflective teaching and teacher education', *Teacher and Teacher Education*, 5:1

Claxton, G. (1999) *Wise Up: learning to live the learning life*, Stafford: Network Educational Press

Edwards, A. and Collison, J. (1996) *Mentoring and Developing Practice in Primary Schools: supporting teacher learning in schools*, Buckingham: Oxford University Press

Furlong, J. and Maynard, T. (1995) *Mentoring Student Teachers: the growth of professional knowledge*, London: Routledge

Jones, M. (2001) 'Mentors' perceptions of their roles in school-based teacher training in England and Germany' *Journal of Education for Teaching*, 27:1, 75–94; available at: http://www.EBSCOHost.com (accessed October 2011)

Maynard, T. and Furlong, J. (1993) 'Learning to teach and models of mentoring', in McIntyre, D., Hagger, H. and Wilkin, M. (eds) *Mentoring: perspectives on school-based teacher education*, London: Kogan Page

McIntyre, D., Hagger, H. and Wilkin, M. (eds) (1994) *Mentoring: perspectives on school-based teacher education*, London: Kogan Page

Rodgers, A. and Keil, V. (2007) 'Restructuring a traditional student teacher supervision model: fostering enhanced professional development and mentoring within a professional development school context', *Teaching and Teacher Education*, 23, 63–80; available at: http://www.sciencedirect.com (accessed October 2011)

Tang, S. Y. and Chow, A. W. (2007) 'Communicating feedback in teaching practice supervision in a learning-orientated field experience assessment framework', in Teacher Development Agency (TDA) (2007) *Standards for the Award of Qualified Teacher Status*, London: TDA

*Teaching and Teacher Education*, 27, 1066–85); available at: http://www.sciencedirect.com (accessed October 2011)

# Endnote

We, as a team hope that you have found the chapters in this book thought provoking and that you feel more secure about the reasons for taking the actions that you do when teaching. If, as we have suggested, you realize that teachers have many choices to make as practitioners then we have succeeded in our purpose. We all work within certain parameters but, by reflecting and responding to the small events in your classroom, you can develop your own practice and establish a strong professional identity. We hope that you and the children in your classes have successful and engaging learning experiences.

# Index

accountability 59
action research 122–3
active learning 19, 20
activities 4
    creative 23
    language-learning 55
additional needs 7
adults 8, 111
*All Our Futures* 59
*Arrival, The* 62
art 87–9
    education 88
    lessons 87
    product approach 89
artistic creation 24
artists 88
arts 23
artworks 87
assessment 32, 43
    formal 14
assistants 9
Audit Commission 7
autonomy 114

behaviour 111
    management 111
Blunkett, David 9
British Council
    International School Award 94
Browne, Anthony 61
buddying 9
built environment 23–5
Burningham, John 61

Callaghan, James 117
    speech at Ruskin College 117

case studies 127
centralized directives 122
centralized guidance documents 122
Centre for Literacy in Primary Education
    67
child development 98
*Children We Teach, The* 111
ChildWise 84
classroom assistants *see* assistants
classroom culture 76
classroom practice 121
classroom research 125, 127
closed questions 73
cloze procedure 12
Coe, Sebastian 79
cognitive activity 61
cognitive challenge action 13
cognitive development 40
collaborative interaction 13
*Come Away from the Water, Shirley* 61
competencies 45
competition 78, 79
compliance 114
conductivity 32
confidence 113, 115
conflict resolution 95
conformity 114
contextualized learning 69
Council for Learning Outside the
    Classroom 37
creative activity 23
creativity 34–6, 87
cultural diversity 53
culture of dependency 15
current affairs 100–102
    controversial issues 102

curriculum *see also* National Curriculum
5, 8, 15, 16, 23, 83, 89, 111, 113, 118,
122
content 111
geography 104
innovation 125
literacy 59
statutory 87
writing 58

decision making 47
DEMOS 118
Department for Education and Skills
(DfES) 31, 37, 94
Department of Health (DofH) 78
dependency culture 15
*Developing the Global Dimension in the
School Curriculum* 95
developing world 101
Dewey, John 3, 128
DfES *see* Department for Education and
Skills
differentiation 11–14
displays 30–32
diversity 95
DofH *see* Department of Health
dopamine 39
drama 57–9
*Duck, Death and the Tulip* 63
dyadic exchanges 43

Early Years Foundation Stage 53
education
politicization of 4
Education and Skills, Department for *see*
Department for Education and Skills
education system 4
educational literature 126
educational research *see* research
electronic communication 4
elitism 110

empathy 62
employment
terms and conditions 118
English language 53, 65
environmental problems 101
Erlbruch, Wolf 63
e-safety 84
lessons 84
ESRC project 42
ethnic minorities 93
evaluation 125, 126
evaluative feedback 76
Every Child Matters 79
examinations 14, 20
Excel *see* MS Excel
extra-curricular activities 3

Facebook 29
feedback, evaluative 76
*Flower, The* 63
follow-up questions 76
Forest Stewardship Council 37
formal assessment 14
Foundation Stage 95
friendship groups 12
fun 79
fundraising 101

games consoles 4
General Teaching Council 118
geography curriculum 104
global citizenship 95
Google 104
Google Earth 103
graphicacy 104
group collaborative learning 44
group work 44

Hathorn, Libby 63
Health, Department of *see* Department of
Health

health and safety  37
hierarchy of needs  47, 49
higher order thinking  73
human development
   theories  109
human rights  95

ICT *see* Information and Communication
   Technology
images  27–9
imagination  62
Imperial War Museum (IWM)  27
improving practice  125–7
inclusion  7–9, 14
independence  15
independent learners  129
independent learning  15–17
India  28
Information and Communication
   Technology (ICT)  35, 83–6, 103
   knowledge  84
   suites  84, 85
Innocenti, Roberto  62
interactive whiteboard (IWB)  34–6
interactivity  35
interdependence  95
international learning projects  94
international links  94
International School Award  94
internet  28, 34, 84
irony  61
Isaacs, Susan  111
IWB *see* interactive whiteboard
IWM *see* Imperial War Museum

Key Stage 1  61, 95
Key Stage 2  53, 55, 62, 95
*Key Stage 2 Framework for Languages, The*
   54
Key Stage 3  16
Key Stage 4  16

language acquisition  54
language learning  53
   activities  55
learning  4, 19–22, 30, 31, 110, 125
   active  19, 20
   contextualized  69
   group collaborative  44
   independent  15–17
   mathematics  73–7
   out-of-classroom  37–40
   personalized  8
   rote  65
learning dispositions  12
learning environment  42
learning experiences  5, 83
learning opportunities  73
learning outcomes  31, 74, 75
Learning Outside the Classroom Manifesto
   38
learning process  4
learning providers  37
learning theory  20, 98
Level 1  129
Level 2  129
Level 3  129
life skills  3
Light, John  63
linear progression  11
linguistic competence  53
Lippmann, Walter  97
literacy  31, 57, 58
literacy curriculum  59
literature  58

managerialism  114
managers, senior  9
mapping devices  103
maps  103–5
Marsden, John  62
Maslow, Abraham  47, 49
   hierarchy of needs  47, 49

mathematical dialogue  74
mathematical processes  71
mathematics  69–72
    learning  73–7
McKee, David  63
meaning  68
memorization  13
mental health workers  8
mentees  128–31
mentoring
    peer mentoring  9
mentoring process  128–31
mentors  128–31
metacognition  97
metacognitive dialogues  21, 22
mobile phones  84
    technology  103
moon landing  27
motivation  11, 12, 13, 24, 30, 32, 39, 40,
    47, 113
MS Excel  83
MS PowerPoint  84, 85
multicultural society  53
multiculturalism  93–5
multiple narratives  28

National Association for Sport and
    Physical Education  79
National College for School Leadership  9
National Curriculum *see also* curriculum
    11, 16, 72, 83–4, 88, 117
National Curriculum for English  57
National Curriculum for PE  79
National Foundation for Educational
    Research  121
National Literacy Strategy (NLS)  42, 57
National Numeracy Strategy (NNS)  42
National Strategies  122
national testing  69
natural disasters  100, 101
needs, hierarchy of  47

neuroscience  23
New Labour  117, 119
New Opportunity Fund  84
newly qualified teacher (NQT)  128
news *see* current affairs
9/11 *see* Twin Towers
NLS *see* National Literacy Strategy
NNS *see* National Numeracy Strategy
NQT *see* newly qualified teacher
numeracy  31, 74

obesity  78
observation  125, 126
Ofsted  57, 122
open questions  73
oracy  57
outdoor learning  37

partnerships  94
PE *see* physical education
pedagogy  35
peer group  9
peer mentoring  9
peers  17
personal, social, health and economic
    education (PSHE)  84
personalized learning  8
Peters, Richard  109
phonemes  66
phonemic strategies  66
phonic awareness  54
phonics  66
physical activity  78
physical development  79
physical education (PE)  78–80
physiology  23
physiotherapists  8
Piaget, Jean  43
picture books  61
picture fiction  61–3
pictures  62

politicization of education  4
popular culture  4
PowerPoint *see* MS PowerPoint
praise  49
Primary Framework  11, 42, 58
private providers  7
problem solving  69, 71
professional development  129
professional growth  130
professional identity  113–15
professionalism  114, 117–19
    surveys  119
prompts  76
providers, private  7
PSHE *see* personal, social, health and
        economic education
psychology  23, 111
pupil-pupil dialogue  44

Quality Improvement Agency  15
questioning  73–7
    techniques  75
questions  21–2, 73–4
    follow-up  76

*Rabbits, The*  62
reading  66
reading skills  62
realistic mathematics education (RME)  71
Reception Stage  61
reflection  19, 22, 73–7, 125, 126, 128, 129
reflective development  89
reflective practice  110
reflective teacher practitioners  129
reflexivity  127
research *see also* action research  119, 121,
        125
    classroom research  125, 127
researchers  121
resilience  128
resourcefulness  128

reward system  48, 49
rewards  47–9
    withdrawal of  48
RME *see* realistic mathematics education
*Rose Blanche*  62
rote learning  65
Russell, Bertrand  109

satellite navigation systems  103
*Saving Private Ryan*  27
school structures  118
second language learning  53–5
secondary school pupils  48
self  114
self-awareness  127
self-doubt  115
self-esteem  30, 32
self-knowledge  113
self-motivation  47
self-reflection  48
SENCO *see* Special Educational Needs
        Coordinator
Sinclair-Coulthard model  42–3
skills  45
social justice  95
social life  4
social networking  4
social skills  79
socioeconomic status  84
sociologists  110
sociology  23
software  83, 84–5
Special Educational Needs Coordinator
        (SENCO)  9
special schools  7, 8
specialist provision  7
speech and language therapists  8
spelling  65–8
    conventions  67
    development  67
sporting events  79

standards 57
Standards for Teachers 122, 126
statements 7
stereotypes 29, 97–9
  cultural 98
  developmental 98
  negative 99
  social 98
students 130
subject content 35
surveys 121
sustainable development 95
syllabus 11, 13

talk partners 76
talking 42–5
Tan, Shaun 62
targets 31
teacher professionalism *see*
  professionalism
teaching 110, 125
technologies 34, 85
terms and conditions of employment 118
test performance 13
testing 5, 13
  national 69
tests 20
text messaging 65
*Three Little Pigs, The* 62
3Rs 128
times tables 75
trainee teachers 128
trouble-makers 5

*Tusk Tusk* 63
tweeting 65
Twin Towers 27

understanding 73
United Nations Convention on Children's
  Rights 4

values and perceptions 95
verbal praise 48
viewpoint 63
*Village in India, A* 27
visual resources 27
visualization 69
*Voices in the Park* 61, 63
Vygotsky, Lev 13, 57, 59

wait time 76
*Way Home* 63
websites 28
WHO *see* World Health Organisation
whole school improvement 125
whole-class teaching 42, 43
Wiesner, David 62
Wilson, Jacqueline 9
word problems 71
working walls 31
worksheets 4
World Health Organisation (WHO) 78
writing 65, 67
writing curriculum 58

*Zoo* 61